Driving Efficiency in Local Government Using a Collaborative Enterprise Architecture Framework:

Emerging Research and Opportunities

Amit Tiwary
Principal Enterprise Architect, Australia

A volume in the Advances in Public Policy and Administration (APPA) Book Series

IGI GLOBAL
DISSEMINATOR OF KNOWLEDGE

www.igi-global.com

Published in the United States of America by
IGI Global
Information Science Reference (an imprint of IGI Global)
701 E. Chocolate Avenue
Hershey PA, USA 17033
Tel: 717-533-8845
Fax: 717-533-8661
E-mail: cust@igi-global.com
Web site: http://www.igi-global.com

Library of Congress Cataloging-in-Publication Data

Names: Tiwary, Amit, 1960- author.
Title: Driving efficiency in local government using a collaborative enterprise architecture framework : emerging research and opportunities / by Amit Tiwary.
Description: Hershey, PA : Information Science Reference, [2017]
Identifiers: LCCN 2017001537| ISBN 9781522524076 (hardcover) | ISBN 9781522524083 (ebook)
Subjects: LCSH: Local government. | Government productivity. | Organizational effectiveness.
Classification: LCC JS78 .T59 2017 | DDC 352.3/75214--dc23 LC record available at https://lccn.loc.gov/2017001537

This book is published in the IGI Global book series Advances in Public Policy and Administration (APPA) (ISSN: 2475-6644; eISSN: 2475-6652)

British Cataloguing in Publication Data
A Cataloguing in Publication record for this book is available from the British Library.

Advances in Public Policy and Administration (APPA) Book Series

ISSN:2475-6644
EISSN:2475-6652

MISSION

Proper management of the public sphere is necessary in order to maintain order in modern society. Research developments in the field of public policy and administration can assist in uncovering the latest tools, practices, and methodologies for governing societies around the world.

The **Advances in Public Policy and Administration (APPA) Book Series** aims to publish scholarly publications focused on topics pertaining to the governance of the public domain. APPA's focus on timely topics relating to government, public funding, politics, public safety, policy, and law enforcement is particularly relevant to academicians, government officials, and upper-level students seeking the most up-to-date research in their field.

COVERAGE

- Government
- Law enforcement
- Political Economy
- Politics
- Public Administration
- Public Funding
- Public Policy
- Resource Allocation
- Urban Planning

IGI Global is currently accepting manuscripts for publication within this series. To submit a proposal for a volume in this series, please contact our Acquisition Editors at Acquisitions@igi-global.com or visit: http://www.igi-global.com/publish/.

The Advances in Public Policy and Administration (APPA) Book Series (ISSN 2475-6644) is published by IGI Global, 701 E. Chocolate Avenue, Hershey, PA 17033-1240, USA, www.igi-global.com. This series is composed of titles available for purchase individually; each title is edited to be contextually exclusive from any other title within the series. For pricing and ordering information please visit http://www.igi-global.com/book-series/advances-public-policy-administration/97862. Postmaster: Send all address changes to above address.

Titles in this Series

For a list of additional titles in this series, please visit:
http://www.igi-global.com/book-series/advances-public-policy-administration/97862

Handbook of Research on Emerging Business Models and Managerial Strategies in the Nonprofit Sector
Lindy Lou West (Griffith University, Australia) and Andrew Worthington (Griffith University, Australia)
Business Science Reference • ©2017 • 509pp • H/C (ISBN: 9781522525370) • US $245.00

Ideological Messaging and the Role of Political Literature
Önder Çakırtaş (Bingol University, Turkey)
Information Science Reference • ©2017 • 317pp • H/C (ISBN: 9781522523918) • US $175.00

Therapeutic Jurisprudence and Overcoming Violence Against Women
Debarati Halder (Centre for Cyber Victim Counselling (CCVC), India & Unitedworld School of Law, India) and K. Jaishankar (Raksha Shakti University, India)
Information Science Reference • ©2017 • 344pp • H/C (ISBN: 9781522524724) • US $230.00

Public Sector Entrepreneurship and the Integration of Innovative Business Models
Mateusz Lewandowski (Jagiellonian University in Kraków, Poland) and Barbara Kożuch (Jagiellonian University in Kraków, Poland)
Business Science Reference • ©2017 • 309pp • H/C (ISBN: 9781522522157) • US $190.00

Handbook of Research on Citizen Engagement and Public Participation in the Era of New Media
Marco Adria (University of Alberta, Canada) and Yuping Mao (California State University Long Beach, USA)
Information Science Reference • ©2017 • 503pp • H/C (ISBN: 9781522510819) • US $265.00

Global Perspectives on Development Administration and Cultural Change
Gbenga Emmanuel Afolayan (Murdoch University, Australia) and Akeem Ayofe Akinwale (University of Lagos, Nigeria)
Information Science Reference • ©2017 • 277pp • H/C (ISBN: 9781522506294) • US $170.00

For an enitre list of titles in this series, please visit:
http://www.igi-global.com/book-series/advances-public-policy-administration/97862

IGI GLOBAL
DISSEMINATOR OF KNOWLEDGE

www.igi-global.com

701 East Chocolate Avenue, Hershey, PA 17033, USA
Tel: 717-533-8845 x100 • Fax: 717-533-8661
E-Mail: cust@igi-global.com • www.igi-global.com

Table of Contents

Foreword

There is a direction within governments across the globe to provide an increasing number of services using digital technologies. This is driven, in part, due to the changing expectations of citizens, a growing demand for services across 24x7 and 365 days per year formats, and the cost of these services in their traditional form. This trend has driven the concept of "Smart Government" whereby services are intelligently designed to take advantage of technology. This includes relatively recent technologies (such as Big Data, Cloud and the Internet of Things).

This in turn drives change in the way local government departments need to design their services. Due to information and financial constraints, most of the services are designed in silos and for a particular service offering. Existing enterprise architecture frameworks support the siloes local government departmental have historically utilised. However, these enterprise architecture frameworks need to rapidly change as governments embraces collaboration across departments. For example, various functions of governments such as immigration, social security and health services are regularly collaborating with one another. This interaction requires inclusion within a corresponding Enterprise Architecture for each department. This is referred to as a Collaborative Enterprise Architecture ("CEA").

The adoption of Collaborative Enterprise Architecture Frameworks (CEAF) within current government environments requires careful and focused planning. A big bang approach whereby government departments suddenly move from their current systems to new more holistic systems is unlikely to be successful. The change would preferably be planned and implemented in an iterative approach, where there is an option to resolve a present pressing need without compromising on the future state of architecture. The CEAF provides a mechanism to optimize the use of legacy systems. This approach provides the mechanism to adopt phased implementations of the CEAF. The

CEAF should adopt a pragmatic approach where the end-state is defined, and many phased decisions are taken to achieve this in a planned manner.

The author, Amit Tiwary is an authoritative source, having a sound understanding of Enterprise Architectural principles, and highly relevant experience at such implementations within complex government environments. His book aims to give readers an understanding of the need for Smart Government, and explore how CEAF can help incorporate SOA, cloud computing, mobile technology and enhanced security to facilitate collaboration. In complex environments, the implementation of a well-designed CEAF and its resulting simplification of the ICT environment, may have the added benefit of reducing resource usages on the physical layer of servers and client devices, including power usage. Similarly, this book also proposes high level strategies that are in line with a move towards green ICT.

Kelvin McBride
Public Services, Australia

Preface

Individually, we are one drop. Together, we are an ocean. – Ryunosuke Satoro

The very core of democracy relates to the need for governments to represent their people. However, the organisational structures of governments around the world are inherently anachronistic in this respect. While the separation of the executive into agencies and departments is required, it breeds bureaucracy and inefficiencies.

As resources and duplication of services proliferate, Smart Government offers a great opportunity to contain duplication and use the resources wisely, to provide better services that are more coordinated, faster, and better connected, while reducing the number of contact points between services and agencies.

Current research by Gartner and Harvard Business review (Leinwand, Mainardi, & Kleiner, 2015)[1] indicates that more than 80% of organisations are unable to realise their planned strategy. This is compounded in the public sector as each change in government brings a new set of policies and priorities. The reason for this appears to be a lack of commonality to bind government's vision and roadmap to strategies for seamless implementation of policies. In current government financial allocations, departments compete with each other for a slice of yearly budgets. This encourages a view to the short term and, in most cases, applying tactical solutions to organisational or social issues.

Local governments are beginning to provide a number of services using digital technology, driven by increasing costs of providing services in their traditional form, as well as the fact that many services benefit from 24x7 digital platforms. This concept, called Smart Government, refers to intelligently designing services to take full advantage of technology.

This changes how local government departments previously designed essential services. Due to information and financial constraints, most services were designed in isolation, or silos, and for a particular service offering. Existing Enterprise Architecture Frameworks (EAFs) support the silos of local government's departmental requirements. However, the EAF needs to change rapidly as government embraces collaboration across departments. For example, various functions of government such as immigration, social security, and health services regularly collaborate with one another. This requires corresponding enterprise architectures in each department, referred to as a Collaborative Enterprise Architecture (CEA).

Further development and formalisation of common capabilities across local government departments will enable development of shared services that meet citizen requirements at a single portal. Many local governments in Australia and across the globe have planned to do this, because it provides efficient and cost-effective services. CEA ensures that information is shared securely and privately, and reduces the need to reinvent the wheel across all departments. For example, technologies such as Cloud computing can enable simultaneous deposit and withdrawal of shareable information by various departments in public/private formats, shared within multiple departments without replicating information in the silo systems of each department. CEA will facilitate providing each department with common information about the residents, locations, and objects within their system. Currently, this information may not be shareable because of varying formats and no unique identifiers to connect the information. This is an era of collaboration more than competition. In fact, this modern business era is particularly adept at using information and communication technologies (ICT) to capitalise on global opportunities to collaborate.

This book aims to give readers an understanding of the need for Smart Governments and a Collaborative Enterprise Architecture Framework (CEAF). It draws upon the author's personal experience in successfully implementing a Smart Local Government framework for a major government sector, while addressing the prevalent internal and external security risks.

The CEAF will provide the advantages of using advancements in communication, security, and cloud-computing technology. In this era of disruptive technology, an enterprise architecture framework needs refining to accommodate collaboration. A study of the key elements of a CEAF would reduce resource usage based on physical layer of servers and client devices (optimisation of the infrastructures or databases), especially power usage. Similarly, it will propose high-level strategies to attain green information and communication technologies (ICT). The book will explore how CEAF can help incorporate Service Oriented Architecture (SOA), cloud computing, mobile technology, and enhanced security to facilitate collaboration. This will offer organisations abilities to publish and subscribe to data, information, knowledge, and intelligence services.

A CEAF can also help ameliorate the following issues by incorporating emerging technologies within collaborations:

- **Trust:** Each organisation will need to deposit information the collaborating organisations can trust, based on quality parameters. The organisation also must comply with the withdrawal rules.
- **Timelines:** Deposited information must be as current as expected by the receiving process.
- **Delivery of Information:** Information must be delivered in the format consumable by the subscribing organisations. Information that needs multiple translations before becoming Collaborative Intelligence (CI) information will make organisations reluctant to adopt this method of sharing.
- **Cost and Resources Required for Establishing Collaborative Intelligence (CI) Platforms:** The approach to implementing CI must consider cost and benefit. If costs are prohibitively expensive, organisations will revert to old Business Intelligence (BI).
- **Legislative and Contractual Framework:** Organisations must develop a framework to quickly define the contracts required for information sharing.
- **Security:** This is a key concern regarding any published information. Information should be context driven by the security processes, so that only those with access to the information can view it.
- **Lack of Uniform Rules:** A lack of uniform rules and legislation for sharing personal information will impede creation of CI. In various countries, legislation for personal information sharing differs.
- **Lack of Context-Sensitive Information:** Discriminating between competitive and collaborative information that can change from time to time and place to place must be possible.

The proposed CEAF will allow government departments to share budgets, resulting in better solutions for the whole government. Similar current initiatives across government departments are limited to either the level of procurement "economy of scale," or a superficial collaboration necessitated by required information exchange among various departments of government. As envisaged in this work, the CEAF can be defined as the link between the government strategy and the corresponding capabilities and technology assets of the whole-of-government in action.

Needless to say, the collaboration required among a government's many enterprise applications is substantial. The impact of one decision at one point in time on many other aspects of the business requires analysis that includes statistical (predictive) analytics and sentiment analytics.

This book argues that a fundamental change permeates governments. A palpable shift from purely "cost-centred" decision making to that of "whole-of-government" requires in turn extensive electronic and mobile collaboration. Such collaboration diametrically opposes looking inward to departmental priorities. Perhaps the rapid growth in information and communications technology is providing the impetus for this shift. The rapidity of global communications has certainly influenced the worldview of leadership—namely, that collaboration is a much better way of providing necessary services efficiently and effectively to citizens, and is also an intelligent way of looking at governments. The open-data initiatives will require a higher level of cooperation within and among government departments.

Below are some of the ways in which a group of organisations can achieve a CEAF:

- Define and share information that would otherwise remain in silos and lead to repeated effort by individual organisations (context-based information sharing). The information sharing is governed by the context of the request and also its security level, based on privacy or departmental sensitivity.
- Keep information current and reliable for use by all collaborating organisations.
- Trust and agreements—both physical and electronic—must go beyond geographical boundaries and regions.
- Create organisational dashboards consisting of multiple-organisation performance, rather than just the CEO dashboard for an individual organisation, so as to provide a succinct view of the collaborative effort.
- Share lessons learnt by one organisation with all other collaborating organisations. This will not only enable reduction of overall wastage, in terms of anticipating and solving problems; it also has security and health implications (e.g., sharing of information on perpetrators and/or diseases across borders and regions). This sharing of lessons in an intelligent way is true collaboration that can occur despite competition.

- Ascertain availability of "like minded" organisations across the world that would like to collaborate by sharing data, information, and knowledge. This can include organisations within a vertical and/or a horizontal line of business.
- Use Web communications technologies (including Web Services and corresponding Service Oriented Architecture) to enable making services available across collaborating organisations.
- Set up legal and compliance structures to safeguard the intellectual property of the collaborating organisations.

Global customers are interested in a holistic end result, not in the individual processes that make up the end result. Collaborative Intelligence leads to service creation, as well as creation of customer groups that can form a dynamic structure to source and provide services within the collaboration.

Many practical aspects of the discussion in this book emanate from work carried out by the author. Coming from the breadth of consulting experience and the depth of industrial research, the material in this book promises to be of value to both business and academics. The author strongly believes this will be a valuable addition to the repertoire of thought processes around Smart Governance, Enterprise Architecture, and Business Intelligence; and that it will provide organisations with much-needed insights into how these technologies can be used in and by business.

ORGANISATION OF THIS BOOK

The book is organised into five chapters. A brief description of each of the chapters follows.

Chapter 1: Key Enterprise Architectural Challenges in Local Government

This chapter discusses the limitations of current architecture frameworks for transitioning restrictive and old IT infrastructure and services, in order to adopt new technology. In addition to the technological challenges, the financial resources are limited in local government departments, and lack of whole-government planning and adoption of technology results in disparate solutions. This chapter identifies the key challenges and risks that local governments face, and the inefficient use of resources that leads to inadequate services.

Chapter 2: Key Elements of CEAF

This chapter explores key components that exemplify the challenges of trust, timeliness, delivery of information, and the sustainability of the CEAF in the context of environmental issues.

Chapter 3: Adopting CEAF

This chapter considers how adopting the CEAF can better incorporate technologies in local governments, and discusses the steps required for adopting CEAF across local governments. This chapter also identifies the risks and issues that could arise using CEAF, and how to mitigate them.

Chapter 4: CEAF Implementation Roadmap

This chapter outlines the future of the CEAF in changing the IT landscape of Smart local governments, and a process for successful implementation.

Chapter 5: CEAF Governance

This chapter outlines the need for governance in adopting CEAF. It recommends the key components of governance required for Smart local governments, and a process for its successful implementation.

Bibliography

This chapter lists a number of references used throughout the book. The list of references is organised based on topics within the book, and will provide readers with further reading or reference material.

REFERENCES

Bregman, P. (2017, January 4). Execution is a people problem, not a strategy problem. *Harvard Business Review.*

Coleman, J. (2017, January 4). The Best Strategic Leaders Balance Agility and Consistency. *Harvard Business Review.*

Davenport, T. H. (2007, December 6). Avoid the extremes. *Harvard Business Review*.

Edmondson, A. C. (2011, April). Strategies for Learning from failure. *Harvard Business Review*. PMID:21510518

Favaro. (2015, March 31). Defining Strategy, Implementation, and Execution. *Harvard Business Review*.

Leinwand, P., Mainardi, C., & Kleiner, A. (2015, December 30). Only 8 percent of Leaders are good at both strategy and execution. *Harvard Business Review*.

Martin, R. L. (2015, September 15). Why Talking about Strategy "Execution" is still dangerous. *Harvard Business Review*.

Sull, D., Homkes, R., & Sull, C. (2015, March). Why strategy execution unravels – And what to do about it. *Harvard Business Review*.

ENDNOTE

1 A number of articles discussing the strategy and execution failure are listed in references, strategy failure is a hot topic extensively discussed in many academic books, articles and other forums such as Harvard Business Review. Some of these articles are listed in reference and guidance to further study.

Acknowledgment

I would like to acknowledge my coauthor of many papers and friend, Dr. Bhuven Unhelkar. Dr. Unhelkar is a well-known writer credited with assisting, encouraging, and authoring a number of papers himself.

I also thank my colleague Thomas Santos for assisting with diagrams, and my manager Kelvin McBride with in forwarding this book and assisting in developing these ideas in implementable concepts.

I would like to acknowledge the encouragement and contributions of my wife (Renu), son (Aneesh), daughter (Ayesha), and son-in-law (Ayush) for their help and encouragement throughout the process of writing this book.

Chapter 1
Key Enterprise Architectural Challenges in Local Government

ABSTRACT

The many enterprise applications of government require a substantial level of collaboration. The impact of one decision on other aspects of the business requires analysis, including statistical (predictive) analytics, sentiment analytics, and cultural and skills analytics.Further, the shift from purely cost-centered decision making to that of "whole-of-government [1] is palpable. Accordingly, extensive electronic and mobile collaboration is required, even though such collaboration is counterintuitive to the mindset of prioritising according to departmental policies. In addition, the challenges governments face range from the time taken to approve an initiative, considering the complexity of processes, to its organisational structure and ever-changing technology in this age.

GOVERNMENT TYPES

There are many systems of government. Some vest all power in one person (Absolute Monarchy), while others are "by the people, for the people" (Democracy).

Irrespective of the system adopted, the government structure will comprise multiple layers. The structure could be federal, where the central and state

DOI: 10.4018/978-1-5225-2407-6.ch001

governments share power. In Australia, constitutional power is divided between the state and the federal government, with independent powers bestowed upon each. In this book, *local government* is defined as the combination of state and lower levels of government that handle community needs. The state or territory government defines the powers of the councils, and decides for what geographical areas those governments are responsible. The naming convention for local governments can differ (e.g., state, councils, shires, municipalities), but the state or territory government above controls them.

Local governments legislate through delegated legislation, often dealing with matters of procedure and detail to supplement primary legislation. This is justified primarily on the grounds of convenience and executive expediency—for instance, running community centres, enforcing some laws, governing local schools, and bearing responsibility for public works such as water and garbage pickup. Councils are better placed to make amendments more quickly, enabling greater flexibility and ease of change in structure, laws, or funding, as need arises. This is important when rules with special relevance for a group, industry, or trade need changing. If the local group and the government are agreeable to the change, they can amend the laws more quickly. Of course, subordinate legislation cannot implement in some areas, such as matters of appropriation or taxes, rules that have a significant impact on individual rights and liberties, or provisions that would impose obligations on citizens to do or not do certain things.

CHALLENGES FACED BY LOCAL GOVERNMENTS

Local governments must work within geographic boundaries, sharing responsibility with other levels of government. The constitution of the country or its legislative power enables local governments to provide some services. The structure and responsibilities may differ, but for the purpose of this book, the key objective of local government is to provide nominated services to its constituents based on a pre-defined method of revenue collection. Local governments are moving to provide services using digital technology, driven by the increasing cost of developing and implementing services using current solution development methodologies. Moreover, citizens demand better services that use digital platforms in 24x7 formats. This concept, referred to as *Smart Government*, stipulates services intelligently designed to make use of technological advantages. This includes recent technologies, such as Big Data, the Cloud, and "Internet of Things (IoT)". IoT is defined as collaboration of

Figure 1. Challenges faced by government and impact

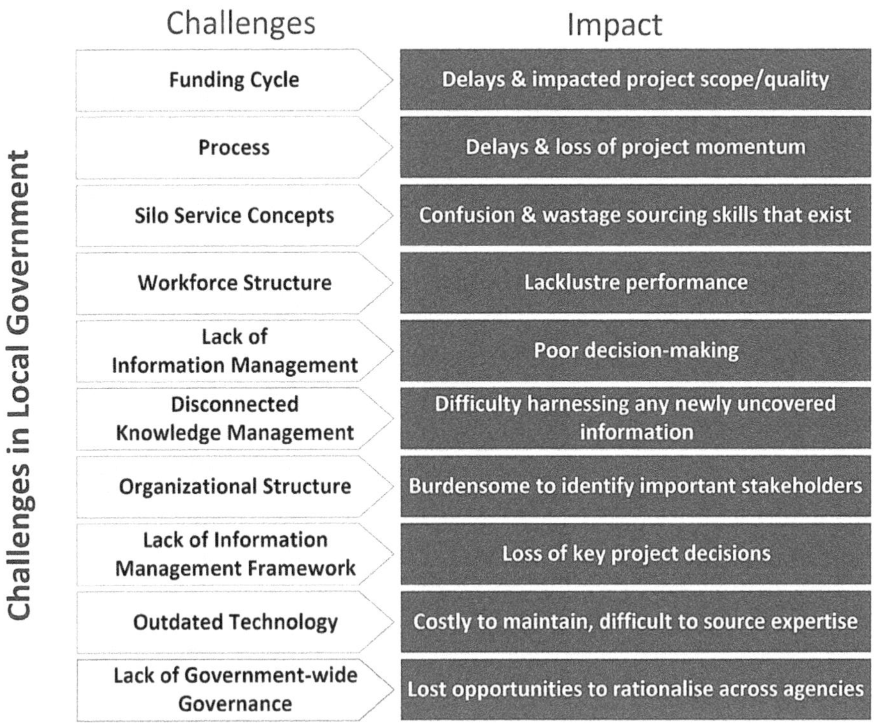

information sharing between traditional information technology systems and smart devices such as mobile phones, operation equipment's with capacity to collect and analyse information (Alaybeyi, Tully, Jones,(2016). The expectation of Smart Government poses the difficult problem to the local government of meeting increasing demand for "Smart Services" within limited budgets, as shown in Figure 1. The government needs a radical overhaul and redesign of its services, so that it can do more with fewer funds available, and meet public needs efficiently and effectively.

With the advent of social media and Web services, citizens are demanding the same service standards from the government. They want to have access to their personal information and details of local civic activities available online. Local governments must manage demand for "open data," where information is available to all, without any restriction by copyrights; and "My Data," as shown in Figure 2, where individual citizen information is available as requested, based on the context of the inquiry. Such changes in services also need to cater to requests locally and globally, requiring processing, classifying, and making available to constituents a significant amount of the data.

Figure 2. My data

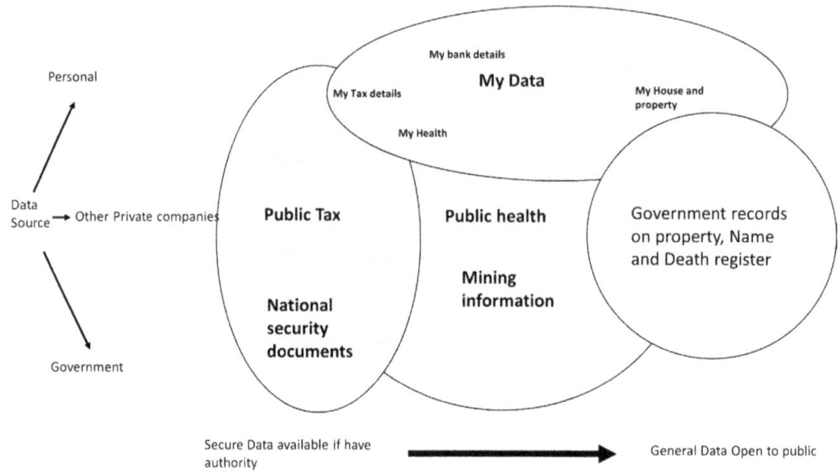

Access to the information also must be managed to differentiate between public and personal information. Employees and citizens will require different levels of access, and properly defining access control is important, as employees will also be end users in their capacity as private citizens. This may require the local government to transfer their organisational IT systems from those that provide "office hour availability" to those that provide "nonstop" services. This includes changes in the system for new processing requirements.

Big data, cloud services, and other new concepts play a major part in changing the value government can provide. The government plays a unique role in realising the financial benefits big data can bring, and it has the power to make changes that can dramatically improve society. It also can encourage private companies to share their data, such as financial analytics. For example, if the government is deciding on developing schools or business precincts, it will require financial and demographical intelligence. The private organisation will have contextual analysis relevant to its business needs. The CEAF could assist private-sector participation in cumulative analysis that utilises entities' intelligence.

Practically speaking, when government is deciding on services in any area, utilities companies, banks, healthcare, and education sectors could share their current statistical and predictive intelligence, and also participate in creating effective services. The concept of private-public collaboration is common in infrastructure development. The CEAF will extend this collaboration across other industry sectors.

Figure 3. Funding cycle and impact on solution selection

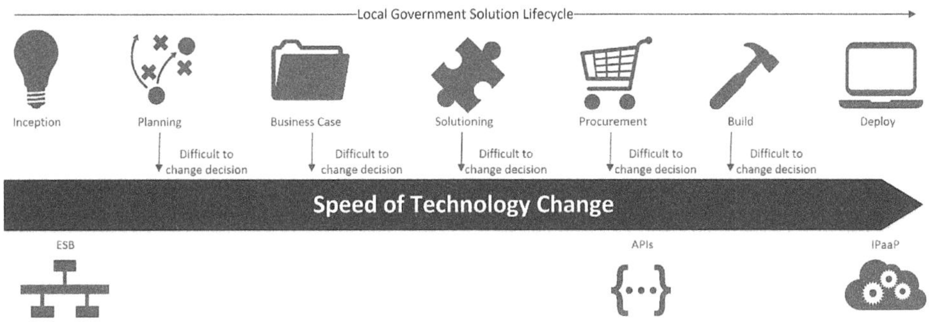

This sharing of data and using it effectively can bring about a transition that overhauls the everyday life of citizens. Government projects (e.g., investment in new cloud technology) are necessary and important to keep up with the advantages technology provides, and also to reduce costs in the long run. Delivering a change at this level, especially where the jurisdiction covers millions of people, is understandably massive and involves many layers and departments. However, such a project done with the right tools and knowledge is feasible and achievable in an acceptable timeframe.

In today's world, knowledge is the key to success. It provides a competitive edge and saves time, effort, and errors, by reusing and building on acquired knowledge. This knowledge can come from the skills and experience of employees, or from the data that has been gathered and analysed.

Business intelligence (BI) can be understood as the creative use of data and information within the organisation in a way that results in new bodies of knowledge applicable in practice. In other words, BI is the use of insightful analysis to make decisions that impact business direction. This is an era of collaboration more than of competition. In fact, this modern business era is particularly adept at using Information and Communication Technologies (ICT) to capitalise on global opportunities for collaboration. Collaborative intelligence (CI) (Unhelkar & Tiwary, 2010) takes BI further, synergising intelligence within and across multiple organisations, to produce actionable value to the collaborators. Such use of BI & CI requires a robust underlying architecture. This architecture is not a single-entity framework, but a combination of various architectures that typically include business, enterprise, and solutions-level architectures. In current digital transformation requiring major changes to systems, each department is tackling changes to its systems using its own limited budget. This will force each department to go its own way in financing, building, and operating its own systems. Local governments may not have invested in information technology due to resource constraints. Such lack of investment in technology could be termed as *architectural debt* or *foundation debt*. Architectural debt could delay the government's transition from current services to "Smart Government" services. Architectural debt within local governments occur for the following reasons:

- The funding cycle is a periodic activity. Funds might be allocated annually, based on plans for investments required within the department. Missing the annual cycle for investing in new technology could result in a time delay before another opportunity arises to apply for funding. The funding cycle could thus create delays in identifying and investing in new technology.
- Local governments may use very old processes. In some cases, processes formed over centuries ago may still carry some of the historical process debts. They are no longer relevant, and no optimisation has been done all this time. The processes may have a number of activities, authorisations, and approval steps whose complexity and lead times could be reduced.
- Workforce structure in many local governments may not be suitable for the new Smart Government requirements. In most cases, government jobs are categorised as safe and associated with long-term careers. Local governments may have a workforce and organisational structure that is not aligned with the requisite "Smart Government" skills and organisational structure.
- Information Management may be aligned with the organisation's structure, and yet still have some information on paper. The information may be isolated and unavailable to other departments for collaborative use with other data to analyse the future needs of citizens on the whole.
- Knowledge should be readily available for the digital change to succeed. Knowledge Management in the department may refer to undocumented individual knowledge in the heads of employees. In some of the cases, organisations may not have invested in technology that could enable utilising information by converting it into knowledge. Also, geographic boundaries may limit the information. In many organisations, recording devices for the information may be obsolete, such as audio and video tapes. The information is stored for the required retention period (in some cases 99 years). This poses the problem of upgrading the storage

mechanism with the new technology if there is no easy way to transfer the information to new device types.

- Government departments often work as standalone entities, and may run only for jurisdictions for which they are responsible. In many cases, the local governments may be adjacent to each other, providing similar services in different formats. External service providers could be contracted, with differing standards and service-level agreements.
- Technology limitations are prominent in local governments, due to lack of investment in technology. The new disruptive technologies demand organisations to adapt to digital business, but the organisational capability to utilise these advancements may be restricted by current technological landscapes.
- The projects initiated by local governments may fail to clearly define the goals and vision. The business outcomes expected from these projects may be unclear or not articulated. This, in turn, will amass requirements that are not well defined. Sometimes, government procurement processes may limit the solution capabilities to the requirements identified in the purchase process.

FUNDING CYCLE CHALLENGES

Tight budgets, transparency, and accountability are the current constraints of most governments. Governments are required to be transparent and accountable to the taxpayer. Budgets are tight, and each government agency must compete with the resources available. Downward trends in information technology investment by government have appeared over recent years. Maximising value from investments has always been an imperative for governments. They must make recommendations when the mission and financial realities conflict. With increased complexity, the cost of IT failure has become all the more significant. Thus, governance must include vigilance in delivering value for such investments. The assets must be managed tightly, and the project must deliver on the benefit it can bring the organisation.

Though there are many funding models in local government, funds allocated to projects generally reflect the value of the idea or the initiative, the priority of the solution being offered, and the funds available. Funding could be a predefined process, and could have lead time of months (in some cases years) from submission to allocation. Long lead time results in many ideas becoming obsolete by the time resources are allocated. In some cases, due to a limited budget, new technologies are not incorporated into the project. This leads to local governments implementing "yesterday's solutions, tomorrow," and always playing catch up. Furthermore, allocated budgets may not be sufficient when new technologies might require new skills.

The long lead time for funding also creates an environment where departments or projects will demand all funding up front, because of the risk of not getting any more funds in future funding cycles. Prioritisation of projects may also occur in silos, so the opportunity to combine similar projects for joint funding is missed. Outcome-based governance could be the basis for the allocation of project funding, which could develop existing capabilities but with different implementations. The projects must constantly be realigned with any technological changes. The funding cycle also demands prior completion of full business requirements. This requires much effort in developing business cases for the financing of initiatives. The cumulative effort just to create the business case could exceed the cost and time for the implementation. In some cases, departments will devise creative methods for implementation of ideas. The budget allocation could be influenced by what will increase decision makers' popularity, and distribution of resources could place them where they may be unnecessary, depriving strategic projects of resources. Developing solutions that meet current tactical requirements and work toward strategic goals requires a pragmatic approach. The use of agile development methods may assist in achieving the goals of tactical solutions with a strategic mindset. Planning is important in adopting this approach, paradoxical to agile methods. Gartner (Tapadinhas, 2016) has discussed "Bi-model" development methods for adopting IT.

Government funding is generally only allocated to project completion and maintenance of the implemented project. Funding may not include amounts for improvements or adoption of new technologies. Accordingly, a foundational piece of required technological change may not be part of the project scope, making the project more complex and ambitious.

Changes in scope over the duration of a project may nullify the objective of the project. The governance and auditing of project-resource usage may be superficial, and project resources could be used for optional requirements. Projects that take more than three years to complete are more likely to be canceled than to succeed, and those with more than 15% staff turnover among key staff are in trouble (Virgo, 2007).

The government often carries out long-term projects, and the same officials might not occupy their seat for the entirety of the project. Once officials leave the project, it might lose traction, and new officials could change its direction, especially if governments and ministers change. Therefore, it is important that programs be divided into smaller projects deliverable within a span of one to two years. Agile methods of working with projects could prove beneficial.

PROCESS CHALLENGES

Citizens are demanding a superior user experience from their government. When taxes and fees are being paid to the government, payers expect it to deliver personalised service and consistency in its processes. To deliver more from less requires a radical overhaul of business processes. However, this does not mean simple automation of processes. Rather, the government should take a fresh look at the entire way the business process works, and redesign it with the end user in mind. Some of the steps in the old process might be repetitious or redundant in the new digital online world. For example, if citizens must enter their personal details many times, restructured and redesigned processes could enable details entered online to be saved in the system without being entered again. This might mean re-examining structures, roles, and operating models. Processing big data and making real-time decisions for next steps in the process might require new data structures.

In such a case, digitisation can cut costs and improve turnaround times immensely. The online data entered not only saves paperwork, but also can connect to other user activities to allow data mining. However, getting to this level of capability might require complex and long projects.

The public sector adds another facet of complexity to managing large projects. As the project involves different divisions, each of the departments could have its own priorities and objectives because of legal, financial, resourcing, IT, or communication issues. Different regulations could apply to differing constituencies; sometimes, political-climate change demands shifts in the direction of the project. If the projects are too big, too complex, or too ambitious, then the risk of failure is significant.

The lack of standards in business processes is a big challenge in the use of big data. Old and new technologies, layered at many points of the system, make it very complex and introduce a number of possible failure points. These all need a proper governing body to ensure that risk of failure is minimised.

The strategic alignment of the project with each of the participating logical groups is imperative for the final success of such a project. This complexity requires constant vigilance, so that the project achieves the critical success factors from each division at each milestone.

Groups need to work with each other to create a holistic approach to a program of development for the entire organisation. This applies especially to data-intense applications and solutions. If communication between divisions is not clear and up to date, each group could end up creating its allocated tasks in a linear fashion and developing its own solutions. This kind of process leads to fragmented governance of projects. Apart from the risks of conflicts, it can also result in building duplicate capabilities. Governance needs to define the outcome of each group's tasks.

Many organisations may not have a defined a data platform to control and manage information effectively. Furthermore, those that have a platform might not have organised repeatability in it. Due to lack of effective Governance, Risk, and Compliance (GRC) in the data space, multiple divisions have their own approach to Information Management. The result will be overlapping and conflicting data structures and usage. This also results in inconsistent investment-decision planning and ad hoc technology investments

SILO SERVICE CONCEPTS

Historically, governments have worked as a network of departments. Nowadays, proper integration is paramount, with a unified system to look at processes, infrastructure, and information management. The absence of such a structure leads in many ways to poor performance and waste of resources. Handoffs between departments can become time consuming and expensive, as can duplication of data, reports, resources, and processes. Each department might have a different procurement supplier; a unified approach could be more economical, and ensure the same standard of service in each department.

Government departments would require a major cultural shift to break down existing barriers. In a digital world, information must be transferred from one department to another seamlessly and quickly. IT systems cannot have barriers due to organisational structure that disconnects divisions; a new structure is required. In current local government organisational structures, roles are distributed across departments, responsibilities are not always clear, and there are no distinct handover points in processes for sharing information and outcomes.

WORKFORCE STRUCTURE CHALLENGES

Workplace conditions in government departments face an interesting challenge. New digital transitions require excellent skills in capacity planning and future planning, as well as up-to-date technical knowledge for implementing new technological solutions. Sustained growth and support of processes and projects require the right mix of skills and capabilities across government departments, and not just in the isolation of a single project.

However, the skills to work in such a dynamic environment are relatively new, and successful private companies can offer generous pay to attract such talent. The government usually cannot offer substantial pay raises, bonuses, or perks, due to human resources (HR) rules and regulations that include limited reward and recognition systems. The digital budget will grow larger in the future, and government HR policies must change to close the gap between private and public hiring rules and regulations.

HR needs to review its policies on skill development, incentives (financial and nonfinancial), performance management, succession planning, and capabilities. Younger generations need to feel empowered about their career, and have chances to improve their skills and opportunities for growth. They must be engaged with the organisation and supported in their long-term career advancement. Giving them opportunities for leadership development and skill advancement will also help build an exciting atmosphere in which younger talent can thrive. This will also enable them to take on future senior-level roles as opportunities become available, leading to smoother transitions within the organisation. Workplace conditions, praising good performance, team building a culture, and providing internal programs to build capabilities and skills that matter, such as on-the-job training, feedback on managing, and risk awareness, are important to attracting employees and retaining talent.

Furthermore, some sections of the society perceive government employees as under challenged and overpaid. Stronger rules providing greater job security than in the private sector make it difficult to deal with poor performers. A popular underlying belief that a government job is "for life" is not a positive atmosphere for employee morale and engagement.

The need for complete transparency and high visibility of all public work is another challenge governments face. Using public money to fund projects likely requires all meetings, decisions, and correspondence to be open to discussion. This creates a new demand for managers to make their employees feel secure, discuss their individual opinions, and manage innovation by ensuring professional and positive public interactions geared toward bringing about a change in public thinking. Government employees need to feel proud of what they do, and public service should motivate them. Long-term goals, values, and impact of projects on civic life should be transparent so that members of the public can see themselves as part of the bigger picture, and enjoy their role.

Apart from the culture, government departments also go through restructuring with each major change of government or leader. They merge, increase capacity, or become fragmented, creating further instability and losing direction for a while. Needless to say, this creates uncertainty in the minds of employees who may find it harder to make a long-term mental commitment to projects.

LACK OF INFORMATION MANAGEMENT

Correct and timely information and data are essential to get to the next step in any online process, especially when discussing real-time decisions. If information systems are not functioning in alignment with strategy, the performance of the organisation suffers. Uniform data across reports, in the form of dashboard reports, requires a centrally accepted approach to information management.

Over the years, legacy systems in government have built ad hoc reports and dashboards in their own format. Eventually, they have a patchwork of reports created and maintained for slightly different purposes, sometimes even using different underlying data with varying definitions. Departments roll up figures in their own way, and in the end, there is a suite of reports that cannot be compared with each other to get to a bigger picture. With no single viewpoint of data, senior management cannot trust the reliability of reports to make decisions. Sometimes, when new data comes in, manual extractions and linkages come up, and parallel systems of reporting operate with overlapping and conflicting data structures and usage. This can also result in inconsistent investment-decision planning and ad hoc technology investments. Sometimes departments control the data as if the group owns it, and get personal about its presentation.

Unless there is uniformity of presentation and rolling up of data, decision makers cannot use information effectively. As real-time instant services are expected, business intelligence needs to be dynamic as well. Blurring the borders between departments enables sharing of information in a timely and useful fashion. The data can only be converted to valuable insights when it is on time, in the right format, and pertinent to the decision. The Key Performance Indicators (KPIs) for different departments often conflict, leading to data reports unusable by other departments. Deciding as time demands on changes in processes to be maintained, reviewed, and realigned requires a unified system.

DISCONNECTED KNOWLEDGE MANAGEMENT

Digitisation works best when old wisdom is paired with new skills. Knowledge is an asset, and if there are means to share it within the organisation, work done once has a more widespread and lasting impact. Knowledge management requires standard processes for creation, organisation, and retrieval of knowledge. Technology selection is an important decision, because IT is an enabler for building a knowledge-sharing culture.

Many technologies are available to help organisations create a knowledge repository. However, they are expensive, and focus on the establishment of a repository, rather than promoting interaction. Employees working in these processes not only gain strong domain knowledge, but also develop heuristics to reduce turnaround time and improve productivity. These heuristics reside in the minds of employees, and when they move to new roles, the organisation might lose their knowledge.

It is imperative for an enterprise to have knowledge about its internal and external capabilities. This insight helps the company reuse its resources, and makes it aware of its winning capabilities in the external market. Whether it is real-time information or knowledge that has been built over time and experience, both assets are needed for a project to be successful, timely, and within budget. Employees should have easy and quick access to knowledge that can help them resolve their issues. Sharing information requires proper technology, processes, and management support, so that employees can use it and buy into the project.

The knowledge in the heads of hundreds of employees is tough to share across locations and divisions. In a government organisation, there are many specialists with varying expertise. Making the combined knowledge of this expertise readily accessible to others could put the agency in a competitive and advantageous position. Employees should also have access to knowledge-management systems that encourage them to share best practices and access critical information in timely fashion. Such systems also must ensure that all documents are kept up to date.

Regulatory agencies also face the challenge of workforces dispersed across multiple offices and geographies. These employees can easily find themselves feeling disconnected, which can ultimately drive them to change employers. Regulatory agencies should provide knowledge-management systems, collaboration tools, and other online networks and communities to keep field forces connected. The importance of knowledge sharing is evident from the recent emphasis on business analytics, where harnessing existing knowledge is crucial for obtaining insights to enhance organisational competitiveness.

The following are challenges emanating from lack of structured information and knowledge-management frameworks:

- **Lack of Useful Tools:** Information Management (IM) tools provide necessary confidence, especially to line managers, that they will be able to retrieve data and analytics as and when needed. However, a lack of tools that not only analyse information, but also make it available, results in managers keeping their own copies of the data and analytics. Considered in the context of Big Data technologies, this is a high-risk scenario, demanding attention to the operational procedures as well as the centralised data infrastructure. In fact, developing in-house capability to support and promote the use of tools consistently is a vital element of Big Data technology strategies.
- **Business Classification Scheme Not Implemented:** Organisations face significant challenges about the management of unstructured information. These problems are further exacerbated when combined with hard-copy documents, and files and electronic records not on any network.
- **Lack of Digitisation Capability:** Digitisation offers great opportunities for organisations to move away from physical record keeping. Big Data creates further opportunities to search, find, use, and correlate siloed data based on physical records. However, an organisation's information-management immaturity and critical dependencies on legacy data may cause failure to undertake digitisation projects quickly enough.
- **Inadequate Infrastructure:** Poor network performance, a lack of storage-capacity planning, and slow reaction to technology shifts/ opportunities has significantly hampered many an organisation's abilities to take advantage of advances in technology. For Big Data and analytics, infrastructure solutions require a careful strategic approach to capitalise on cloud-based storage and analytical opportunities.

- **Security:** Security of data and information is of further importance in Big Data because of the need and opportunities to share data and analytics. A dynamically updated profile for a suite of users and the organisations they represent becomes a must. The levels of security should enable information use by collaborating organisations for agreed-upon purposes and, at the same time, safeguard the information from any malicious use.
- **Performance:** The speed and accuracy of services with the large volume of Big Data initiated transactions will depend on their interfaces and the resources. While Solution Oriented Architecture (SOA) provides necessary technical integration, performance remains a major challenge in adopting Big Data for real-time use in organisational decision making.
- **Metrics and Measurements:** The success of adopting Big Data will depend upon the value it adds to the organisation. The balanced scorecard approach bases overall performance measurements on collective measurements of financial items, internal processes, learning and growth, and customer satisfaction. This approach is suggested where organisations could define the financial measures on which they will base Big Data investments.
- **Incomplete Single Data Models:** This results primarily from organic growth—there is no single and complete data model within most organisations. While there are Master Data Management (MDM) initiatives, these take an unduly long time and come with high costs. Business stakeholders feel that they are losing out on Big Data technology advantages, due to lack of consistent and unified Master Data. While many data models exist, they are not all aligned, and in some cases they conflict with each other. A typical example of such a data-model mismatch is multiple instances of the same customer across three or four different databases. Multiple databases containing the same fundamental information (e.g., names, locations) create a nightmare for maintenance, as well as operational use. Data held in different sources cannot be matched if it does not share a unique identifier, or the same properties or definitions. Therefore, data cannot be integrated or validated to support a single source of truth, such as a single view of an entity. This poses a major problem in adopting Big Data for business use, since the standard information received externally (e.g., name and address) cannot refer to organisational data, and will elevate the problem of duplication of data.

- **Inadequate Impact Analysis:** Understanding data risks and the impact of change across the data architecture involves complex and lengthy analysis. Decisions often are based on inadequate analysis, are not properly informed, and have unintended consequences costly to remedy. This impacts information sharing between agencies, due to security or sensitivity of information. Reporting adequately also becomes complex, due to distribution of information across different systems or agencies.
- **Inadequate Reference-Data Management:** Reference data consists of data that gives context and meaning to other data. This data can be referenced not only for reuse, but also to enhance quality. Everyday users do not capture it, and it is always a constrained set of well-defined and well-understood values, with no overlap with other reference data. Typical examples are postcodes, dates, policies on bank accounts, and parameters for insurance claims, considered as business rules, procedure status codes, gender codes, or similar references. As with other data, sharing reference data to the fullest extent possible maximises its value.
- **Lack of Integration:** Data entry into information systems can involve significant overhead, with repeated data entry or inadequate controls over data entry resulting in degraded data quality.
- **Failure to Realise Data Value:** In many organisations, the value of the organisation's data is not well understood, and opportunities to exploit the organisation's information for strategic use are not optimised. This issue is further aggravated with Big Data because the data itself is highly complex and dynamically changing. Seeing the value of the data occurs in the phase after the data is understood "as is." Information taken cumulatively within organisations could assist in developing new services and innovation options. Government organisations could use the approach adopted by the private sector, of learning from both success and failures to develop better services. In many cases (e.g., NASA), current innovation in the industry slowly tickles down to daily use.
- **Information Management Framework (IMF) Absent:** Information is collected, recorded, created, and used in many different forms and for multiple purposes. However, without an effective overarching IMF, information is at risk of being dealt with in an ad hoc manner.

ORGANISATIONAL STRUCTURE CHALLENGES

As previously stated, government has historically worked through separate departments with little information flow between them. This must change to empower a digital revolution. Technology can be used to create knowledge storehouses; however, technology-based information sharing requires plenty of individual participation. In the absence of incentives, there might be very little participation in sharing this knowledge, rendering the platform ineffective. Structured and unstructured information must be available in the context of the knowledge and information requirements of different groups. Managing and ensuring that information and knowledge are relevant and current requires online portals and knowledge repositories. Unless information is reviewed and its lessons applied all the time, it is not of much use.

Employees often do not want to share their knowledge, feeling that it is their competitive edge. There might be new technological tools for sharing it, but unless the culture and initiatives of government departments promote such sharing, actual knowledge transfer might not take place. Some of these initiatives might include establishing interest groups, and rewarding and publishing knowledge articles. It is important to have top- and middle-manager buy-in, as they are responsible for creating an information-sharing framework to facilitate timely and context-based information and expertise sharing. Knowledge is about not only the file locations or the process used, but also the experience gathered after having worked on a process for some time—for example, knowledge of a geographical location and its intricacies that can help in building and designing roads and highways. This experience takes time to build, and is the key factor in competitive advantage. Accordingly, it must be documented and shared to assist in learning from mistakes. This helps to create a common understanding across diverse locations, and to bring about a feeling of connection with employees that might belong to various divisions.

Minimising the issues in transition to a digital world requires restructuring. The Australian Government, like many around the world, has a complex and occasionally overlapping structure, operating as separate units at the centre. Departments operate relatively autonomously within spending limits and policy guidance agreed upon at the centre. Multiple agencies might have differing priorities or inconsistent business processes. Finding the right way to optimise the structure, scale, and operating model of the government, without creating the disruption and uncertainty of constant organisational change, is important in both achieving fiscal consolidation and ensuring the effectiveness of public services. This raises questions about the structure of central government, the operating model between the centre and departments, and how best to eliminate duplication and redundancies between and within different levels of government. However, whatever level of devolution and decentralisation is chosen, the government can act to reduce duplication of budgets, structures, and resources between and within levels of government.

LACK OF GOVERNMENT-WIDE INFORMATION MANAGEMENT FRAMEWORK

An Information Management Framework (IMF) enables understanding of information needed to support business functions; how and when the business uses the information; who owns the information; where that information is stored; the format in which it must be kept; its security classification; and who can access it. Although government departments use the same information entities, the lack of an enterprise information management framework results in process failure, as transparent processes cannot be defined to improve the quality of data and integrate it with systems. In the case of using hybrid data, security and privacy are major concerns, but processes to ensure tight security and privacy of data cannot be defined. Data cannot be adequately aligned to the needs of the business to provide timely, contextual information. All disparate information from various systems becomes difficult to integrate. There is no enterprise view of information, and thus governance also becomes difficult. Not knowing where to fetch the information required makes the cost of retrieving information prohibitive.

OUTDATED TECHNOLOGY

Meeting the new challenges faced by governments across the globe requires agile systems and, in turn, a transformation of the current architecture to realign with new technology capabilities. Security systems also will need updating with the arrival of Big Data, and processes will need redefining. Long lead times to develop a system are no longer viable. There is time for a quick prototype, with reiterations until a useful system is built. This approach is very different from the linear method of "waterfall" system building. There is a need to develop an Enterprise architectural system that embraces old and new. This new method is called the "Bi-model" approach to developing systems with agile and waterfall methods.

Another deterrent to taking up new technology is the time spent on legislative checks, risk assessments, and regular updates in laws and rules. The government must be fully accountable, requiring organisational and technological risk evaluations, continually evolving legislation (with new governments), and enforcing compliance. Ensuring that these laws are being satisfied—especially when they cross many government organisations—requires many checks. This is time-consuming, laborious, and discourages take up of new technology.

LACK OF GOVERNMENT-WIDE GOVERNANCE

Governance is the overall management approach that monitors and controls projects in organisations, so as to deliver value and not lose sight of the big picture. Governance must understand both the strategy and the limitations of the organisation, in order to make sensible, cost-effective, and appropriate decisions.

Governance is usually top down. The organisation can approve the priorities of the business, based on its capabilities, when approval comes from the decision-makers and owners of the organisation. Effective governance relies on a body that comprises both business and technical decision makers of the organisation. It is a two-way learning process between executives (senior leadership teams, publicly selected legislatives and ministers) and government employees. A good governing body can help steer projects in the right direction, especially when conflicts arise. At the same time, governance is also about continuously improving, tracking, and monitoring its model, so that it delivers better results each time.

Government projects face many hurdles, and their governance has its own challenges. Governance also advances confidence in the business if it is done with responsibility and direction. Some of the reasons government projects need governance include:

- **Weak Business Case:** The desired outcome and its benefits to the organisation are not stated clearly. The ROI on the project and its ability to take the organisation closer to its strategic goal must be articulated convincingly to get traction from the senior team.

- **Expected Outcome of the Project Is Not Stated Clearly:** If the desired results are ambiguous, each group can interpret them differently, and the project will not deliver the result that solves the puzzle of the department's final state.
- **Senior Management Is Not Convinced of the Project Benefits:** Unless top and middle management buy into the project, enterprise-wide support essential to a huge overhaul of the agency will not be achieved.
- **Ineffective Gateway Reviews:** When the project passes from one team to another, the reviews should have clear deliverables accepted by both the delivering and the accepting team.
- **Poor Communication:** The change the organisation wants to accomplish and the pieces of work required to bring it about must be well communicated to the entire department, so that everyone feels involved and ready for the change when it happens.
- **Scope Creep:** In many cases "scope gallop," this must be managed so that the project delivery can occur in time and on budget for the primary goal that initiated it.
- **Poor Stakeholder Agreement:** Conflicts of interest between stakeholders must be managed so that opinions and issues are discussed and a joint agreement reached.
- **Over Projecting Benefits:** This leads to the sentiment of failure when the project does not deliver as promised, when in reality that outcome could not have been reached in any case.
- **Lack of Individual Thinking:** Stakeholders may fail to think individually, going instead with the sentiment of the group. Individual thinking and ideas are necessary for consideration, so that the project as a useful piece of work represents the best use of technology and time.
- **"Big Picture" Is Not Clearly Understood:** The project team needs to know where it fits into the bigger picture of the strategic goal, and what it must deliver to be useful and fruitful. Team members participate more actively when are explained the overall outcome their effort will achieve.
- **Overly Detail Focused:** Decision makers are too involved in the details of the project and cannot see the result clearly. The team that does the detailed work should not be the only one that decides project direction.
- **Lack of Proper Governance Structures:** Projects that fall between two departments are more complicated. If accountability is not clear,

the team building the systems must make their own decisions, which inevitably leads to problems.

Governance should make clear who is responsible for what, and ensure that the parties have the know-how to make the decision. Governance should enhance processes, which in turn helps identify risks up front and enables positioning of adequate controls to ameliorate those risks. In the context of future Big Data technologies, it is vital that these risks be identified quickly and handled efficiently. Big Data technologies provide a full gamut of options and expose the organisation to a suite of uncertainties regarding business and technology strategies and their execution. Governance and risks are a balancing act to ensure achievement of business objectives, both strategic and operational.

If there is a change in the government, the project might not have the same priority or ongoing budget that it had previously. This change in situation must be managed in such a way that the project still delivers value with available resources, and reaches a milestone that can be chosen and extended later. Changing directions of the government should not lead to a waste of the resources invested so far. In such cases, it makes sense to have smaller deliverables, with shorter timeframes and critical success factors intact.

UNDERSTANDING OF THE GOALS

Senior management must understand the result of the strategy crafted and the capabilities needed to achieve the goal. It should also be clear on its current state of capabilities and the gap between the current and the desired states.

In order to achieve the result, there must be many little projects delivering small pieces of work, leading toward the bigger result. They should be like pieces of a jigsaw puzzle that fit to deliver the business outcome as a whole. Each of these little projects must be successful to realise the goals. Some of the reasons for the failure of these projects are:

- **Lack of Understanding Goals and Vision:** Understanding why the project is being done, how it fits into the bigger picture, and what is to be achieved, require clear communication. Otherwise the result might not be the one for which the project sponsor was looking. Projects might be misaligned and not delivering in the direction of the desired goal. A holistic view of all the projects ensures that there is no duplication of work or conflicts of resources. One project should not undo the effects of another, so that benefit to the department as a whole is lost.

- **Not Having the Right Management for the Project:** Failure to have leadership in business, organisational, or technical domains may cause the project to be delayed, lose direction, or deliver late. A project should have a sponsor who will take responsibility for seeing the project through. This sponsor should have the skills and time necessary to perform the role effectively. Apart from the sponsor, the project manager also should steer the direction of the project on the right track, and have the know-how to make people work together to finish the project on time and within budget. Micromanagement or lack of management can cause projects to fail or run out of control.
- **Stakeholder Engagement Issues:** A classic mistake is failure to engage the right stakeholders. The project should be directed toward the desired state by communicating with all stakeholders from its beginning. Their buy-in and view of the final state must be the priority of the program for its eventual success and use. Sometimes the less vocal stakeholders' issues are not addressed, and their needs are not heard. Stakeholders need to remain clear on what is being delivered and how the new technology will be used. Many projects finish on time and on budget, but the capability they have delivered does not get used. This is also a failure of the project.
- **Team Issues:** Every team member's role and responsibility must be clearly understood. There should be enough staff to complete the work, and they should have adequate time to finish it. They should have the Subject Matter Expertise (SME) and skills to do it, and receive training in technical or business domains if needed. Work should be divided fairly; otherwise discontent and demotivation will arise. If projects are delayed, just adding resources might not help finish it in time. The actual issues of the team must be understood and acted upon.
- **Requirement Issues:** These are the details of what is in scope and out of scope. Scope creep should be controlled. Requirements of stakeholders and any additional requests should contribute to reaching the overall goal with an acceptable ROI. Stakeholders with conflicting perspectives and needs could cause dissatisfaction with the result. An agreement about the outcome must be reached beforehand.
- **Estimation:** Those who will do the work should agree to the estimate and be involved in creating it. Estimates should not be cut to secure a contract, and project scope should be clear, with sufficient information

and analysis to make proper estimations. All big and small activities should be considered. Contingency planning for the unknown should be built into the estimate. Assumptions should be documented. A new tool, process, or system does not automatically deliver efficiency, which should be taken into account. The previous performance of projects should be considered before giving the estimate. Estimates should have a range of values to allow for unknown factors. A calendar of upcoming activities will ensure that all work is done and none forgotten.

- **Planning:** Failure to plan the project and its execution in detail is a huge reason projects are unable to deliver as required. Big pieces are divided into smaller pieces of manageable work. While planning, each step should be thought over, or the complexity of the project may not be clear. At the same time, planning each step will clarify the resources in time and skills required. Some buffer should be maintained, and a very tight schedule avoided, to accommodate an unforeseen circumstance. Each team member should be clear on responsibilities, with the workload equally distributed according to skills and priority of the project work. Along with the project manager, team members should be empowered to actively contribute to planning the schedule. This gives a better approximation of project timelines, as the person doing the work will have a better idea of time needed to finish the task allocated. Any training needed should be planned ahead. Culture-change training (the way the end product will bring about the change) should also be considered. If other teams are expected to deliver some work pieces, they should also commit to the timeline, or the schedule will not deliver. User training requirements must be considered as well. The scope of the project can change during its build, but the project should always deliver on the initial intended outcome. Any extra features in scope creep should be considered after looking at benefits and costs.
- **Risk Management:** Failure to see the risks and address them can be avoided if risks are evaluated independent of planning the project. The risk team should not deal with the everyday issues and problems.
- **Architecture and Design:** A pet project should not be prioritised before considering other options and solutions. Poor architecture is hard to maintain and debug. Overall architecture should be considered, and always before individual components are worked on. All requirements, especially performance requirements, must be incorporated before any detailed project work starts. Otherwise, the end solution might not give

the desired business outcome. Over delivery is unnecessary—only such tools as benefit the final result of the project should be considered. Sometimes new tools are required, and time should be allocated for learning.

- **Decision-Making Problems**: People who do not have subject matter expertise make strategic, architectural, and structural decisions. Principal owners of decisions and the process by which they are made should be established. Critical decisions need the right advice, and follow through must occur to ensure the decision was respected. Those who make the decisions must be aware of all the details of issues and keep them in mind. Sometimes difficult decisions are not made because some stakeholders might not be happy with the outcome. Critical decisions should be made after consulting with the group, considering all options, and deciding on the best answer. The people involved should understand all decisions made. Sometimes parts of decisions are never finalised, and this results in confusion.

REFERENCES

Alaybeyi, Tully, & Jones. (2016, May 9). B*uild Your Blueprint for the Internet of Things, Based on Five Architectural Components*. Gartner.

Tapadinhas. (2016, April 12). S*elect the Right Architecture Model for Your Modern BI and Analytics Platform*. Gartner.

Virgo, P. (2007). Why do government projects fail so often? *Computer Weekly*. Retrieved from http://www.computerweekly.com/feature/Why-do-government-projects-fail-so-often

ENDNOTE

1 **Whole of Government:** Describes a fundamental shift in relations between many departments to improve the central strategy, involving major agreements on budgeting, and commitments in time.

Chapter 2
Key Elements of CEAF

ABSTRACT

The existing Enterprise Architecture Frameworks support the silos created by local government departmental requirements. However, as the concept of collaborative government progresses, this architecture will need to change so that it becomes a platform shared across many different services. For example, various functions of government, such as immigration, social security, and health services, regularly collaborate with one another to provide better service, without having many citizen touch points. This requires corresponding enterprise architecture for each department, referred to as a Collaborative Enterprise Architecture Framework (CEAF). The CEAF will provide advantages in the use of advancements in communication, security, and cloud-computing technology. Nowadays, when technological upheaval is imminent, an EAF must be refined and tuned. A study of the key elements of a CEAF would reduce resource usage based on physical layers of servers and client devices (optimisation of the infrastructures or databases), especially power usage. Similarly, it will propose high-level strategies to attain green ICT. This chapter will explore how CEAF can help incorporate SOA, cloud computing, mobile technology, and enhanced security to facilitate collaboration. This will offer organisations a framework for publishing and subscribing to data, information, knowledge, and intelligence services.

DOI: 10.4018/978-1-5225-2407-6.ch002

INTRODUCTION

The very core of democracy relates to the need for governments to represent their people. However, the divided organisational structure of governments around the world is not attuned to providing this service. Execution of various services does need to be managed separately, but if this division becomes more formal, it starts slowing down the system. Red tape creates doubling up of tasks in separate departments, and this creates inefficiency. It is clear from this duplication of resources and services that an opportunity exists for the concept of a Smart Government. Governments can become "smart" through a framework of collaboration applied to existing systems, increasing efficiency and freeing up resources. To implement the collaborative approach, government departments have several choices. They can build from scratch, choose best-of-breed hardware and software products, and integrate themselves; or they can go with a bundled, preintegrated suite. Whatever the choice, it is critical for governments to recognise the full potential of the packages and software they buy. They must realise that their internal software and processes will have been redesigned to get the greatest benefit from these new-era tools. A simple installation will not give them those full benefits, and they might even be worse off if the complete solution and adoption of the new technology has not been thought through from end to end. Knowledge about industry best practices and common IT standards will help ensure sustainable, intuitive ways of addressing citizen and government needs.

To capture the full benefits of digitisation, governments must look for opportunities to improve productivity, collaboration, scale, process efficiency, and innovation. Turning the agency toward digitisation requires transformation of processes and business. Government agencies around the world are under internal and external pressure to become more efficient by incorporating digital technologies and processes into their day-to-day operations.

COLLABORATIVE ENTERPRISE ARCHITECTURE FRAMEWORK

The modern business era is particularly adept at using information and communication technologies (ICT) to capitalise on global opportunities to collaborate.

This chapter intends to give readers an understanding of the need for Smart Governments, and provide them with a Collaborative Enterprise Architecture Framework.

Smart services require a shift in the way local governments design services. Due to information and financial constraints, individual departments develop most of the services with only a particular service offering. This cosmos of complex systems, which changes as business and technology needs change, is supported by the existing Enterprise Architecture Framework (EAF). As departments move toward data sharing and achieving goals together, EAF must incorporate this. For example, transport, trade, agriculture, and tourism can work together to create more jobs and improve economic development of the country, if they can share data on economic development and other activities. Once all the required data from different systems can be integrated in a way that creates a balanced "ecosystem" feeding into each other's requirements and growth, a Collaborative Enterprise Architecture Framework (CEAF) appears. CEAF is multiple organisations sharing business processes and information for a win-win outcome, without compromising their own legislative and departmental requirements. CEAF revolves around the sharing of various information system-related resources in a well-defined context, without compromising organisational responsibilities. These can include exchange of data, information, processes, and knowledge. When multiple organisations, or even departments, share these resources, they move the participating group toward collaboration.

Global planning is underway for further development and formalisation to provide governments with the ability to develop shared services that meet citizen requirements from a one-stop online shop. This provides efficient and cost-effective services.

However, common information may not be shareable because of incongruent formats and a lack of unique identifiers to connect information. CEAF ensures that information is shared securely and within the context of privacy, while reducing the need to reinvent the wheel across all departments. For example, emerging technologies, such as cloud computing, can enable deposits and withdrawals of shareable information by various departments in public/private formats. Such information is stored once and shared within multiple departments, without replicating it in the separate systems of each department, as happens frequently in the current structure. CEAF will support each department with standard information about the residents, locations, and objects within their system.

Sharing and using innovative technology within various departments and governments with CEAF will provide advantages in the use of advances in communication, security, and cloud computing technology. For example, a Citizen identification or digital identity would be required to access all services across government agencies. One agency might develop this service for use across other agencies.

When a higher level of authentication is required (for example, in military services), agencies may require additional steps.

The single "Digital Identity" service will not only save resources across agencies, such as application licenses, infrastructure for the application, and retained citizen information. The single-service concept will also encapsulate customer changes in one place and save multiple agencies' required resources to keep the data up to date. This chapter will explore how CEAF can help incorporate Service Oriented Architecture (SOA), cloud computing, mobile technology, and enhanced security to facilitate collaboration, offering organisations opportunities to publish and subscribe [1]to data, information, knowledge, and intelligence services.

The layers of the organisation that need realignment of all existing and future IT systems are described as:

- **The Presentation Layer:** This layer provides requested information and manages content for the end user. It may require information services replacing current systems and application-driven access. Many organisations utilise an employee portal that manages all access to systems. This will need to change, and the level of access granted will depend on the employee's information needs. Unlike the information required, the system where information is sourced is not available and open to the employee. The interagency exchange will need users' profiles available across the agencies, with authentication and authorisation of information access defined centrally.
- **The Information Layer:** This layer manages all information across the enterprise, using rules and standards to ensure the information is presented in an accurate, timely, and relevant manner. It manages information as an entity that is a state /national asset, shared as needed. The information layer will need realignment to accommodate the aging systems that coexist with the new technology. Financial resources will restrict the modernisation of the systems, based on the funding available. If implemented effectively, the CEAF will provide a modernisation plan for all the agencies' information systems.

- **The Services Layer:** This provides the information from the organisation's systems in a consistent and consumable manner. The CEAF must define the list of all services that will be provided to its user base, consisting of citizens, partners, vendors, service providers, interagencies, and other users. The service layer should be the anchor of the CEAF. It will utilise the information layer to provide context-based services to the user base. The context will be built on the authorisation and authentication of the users.

Alongside the layers of the architecture are two pillars that support the entire architecture: governance, which will be discussed in Chapter 5; and security, embedded within each layer of the architecture in a consistent manner, as well as in statutory requirements, and pervasive across the organisations, especially in a collaborative information-sharing structure.

The new collaborative architecture requires consideration of the following key principles.

Single Data Entry Collection Methods Used for Information Exchange

CEAF success will depend upon information management, where the context of the information is the basis for collecting it in the most efficient way. This collection must be simple, with only a single entry of data. Once entered, data is synthesised and distributed to all systems, (based on Publish and Subscribe). The Publish and Subscribe is commonly used integration method where information provider will define the format and structure of information to be shared called Publish and authorise users can integrate to extract this information called subscribe. It is also important to manage the quantity and velocity of information generated.

The success of CEAF will depend on how organisations cooperate in contributing and sourcing from the services on the CEAF platforms. Global planning for further development and formalisation will provide governments with the ability to develop shared services that meet requirements from one portal. For example, governments around the world, in Asia, India, Europe, and America, are broadly embracing these technologies. Cloud technologies are delivering e-government services, changing the way the consumer behaves, and providing efficient and cost-effective services. If citizens enter their personal data once in an e-form, their information is saved in the system and they

Figure 1. Collaborative enterprise architecture framework

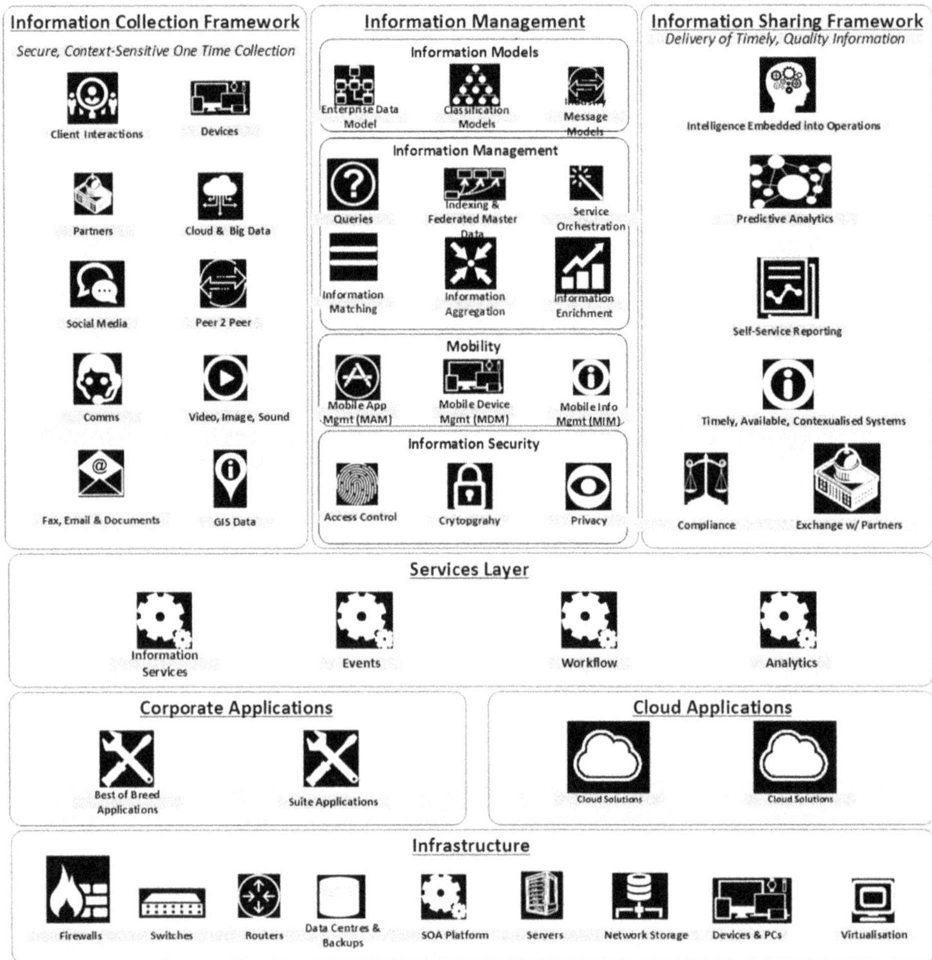

receive a registration number. After that has been processed, the registration number should be all they need for the system to fetch that information. In India, Aadhar Card (a citizen card with biometric authentication) is now in use across all government services, as well as for private organisational services such as banking and utilities transactions.

Governments have invested in developing standards and policies for ICT. These standards are a good start for use in smart service development. Also, the investment in cloud computing and information sharing should follow best-practice guidelines and methodologies, as they will form the basis for the extent of possible future growth. Projects should have to go through reviewing committees, and these practices should undergo continuous evaluations. Such review enforces common standards, rethinks investments, and ensures projects are done within industry-wide accepted standards and guidelines as discussed in the Australin government smart cities plan (Australian government, 2016).

INFORMATION COLLECTION FRAMEWORK

The critical objections citizens will have concern the issues of data protection and privacy. The risks inherent in connecting personal digital information to city operations and the broader smart city partner ecosystem are real. In this resides a remarkable conflict. The ability to identify personal details in the segmentation process, and therefore deliver citizen-centric contextualised services, stands in contrast to the right of privacy, especially when city and citizen data would be potentially orchestrated in city open-data portals and linked to a commercial service environment. Therefore, a data-governance model for smart cities is urgent, because its absence will potentially create a distracting discussion instead of creating clear data value (Australian Government, 2016). The Figure 2 defines the information collection framework.

Many retailers rely on data mining of social media for their media campaigns. So while the technology is available, there is also the question of how much citizens, as consumers, would approve of such situations—very likely less when there is a lack of transparency in how this data will be handled, aggregated, and stored.

Client Interactions

Cities can leverage a variety of different data points from their own internal municipal operations to understand how government and public administration could become smarter and more integrated, often defined as Smart Government in local administration. Connecting municipal data with city-management data, such as public works, public transportation, waste and water utility, and environmental statistics, cities can start to map city-specific information. This can occur either in real time or through management systems—for example, by blending those with information sets obtained through processes or records.

In addition, citizens generate data in various formats. One example of using this data could be to see where public transport is being used (buying tickets behavior), which transport routes are busy, and which parking meters

Figure 2. Information collection framework

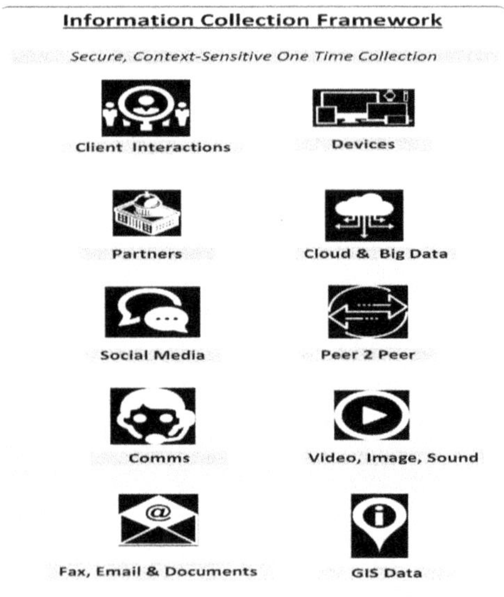

are constantly in use for parking. This can lead to locating traffic congestion and where more public transport or more parking facilities might be needed.

For example, the City of Chicago has built an online app allowing people to report any civic issues such as potholes, sanitation code violations, or streetlight outages. Citizens take the photo, put the location on map, and register the event online at the portal. They can monitor reports online.

This data comes in various forms: email, pictures, or through an embedded text field. Another excellent resource to understand the city's sentiments and events in real time resides in the social web domain, through applications such as social media, Twitter, and TripAdvisor, or in video and picture sharing.

Devices

Various devices in the new technology support the digitisation of the government. Citizens are using multiple technologies such as emails, web, videos, and voice; and various storage media such as servers, hard drives, and mobile devices for their online interactions. Compiling data from all these sources must ensure that privacy and integrity of data are not compromised. This data can either stay in the original repository or be transported. The process of collecting data from various devices and transporting or tagging it is time consuming and costly.

Partners

Using open or pooled data from all businesses in a particular sector, and putting it together with proprietary big data, can help companies develop knowledge and intelligence they could not have acquired with just their data. New research from McKinsey suggests that $3 trillion or more in annual value could arise from the use of open data in applications.(Chiu,Manyika,Kuiken, 2014). The future benefits include using industry-wide benchmarks to assess and compare performance. Examples of using collaborative data for the betterment of society include:

- Since 2000, energy prices have increased by more than 250 percent. Increases in the cost of oil and gas have become the norm, adding to the base cost of a number of other commodities in the market. Technology can improve processes and productivity of reservoirs, as oil and gas exploration are information dependent. Today, with new technology, wells can be created in geological formations that were not feasible before. However, this also raises costs and risk. The approval process for drilling is lengthy, and initial exploration still has a low success rate, raising overall costs. If companies can share information about new drilling methodologies and seismic data, the success ratio of exploration of new oil fields and their operating performance will improve (calculated at the moment at the rate of 50 to 1). Better performance will bring down cost and reduce risk. Governments can develop policies that involve sharing seismic data with a few other companies as part of granting drilling permits, to decrease the number of wells where no significant amount of oil is found, and improve chances of investments leading to best results. Sharing this data among a few interested companies (semi-open data) could produce significant new value in the oil and gas industry. Governments could take the lead in structuring policies for initial drilling licenses that would require sharing of seismic data.
- Sharing data on projected costs and development timetables (through third parties) could establish benchmarks that would reduce per-project costs.
- Shared data that can create benchmarks can also give away a company's position in the market. Competitors will be able to judge how well or how badly the company is doing by the benchmark. Companies

might not want their competitors to know this information. Similarly, social data clearly shows the sentiments of the public, which could be a concern to some consumers; but at the same time, this open sharing also generates discussion and ideas on building new products. Hence, open data has created not only new opportunities, but also a huge gap between decisions regarding privacy and laws about using information.

- Open data, especially government data that can be shared in a machine-readable format, can create tremendous economic value, and improve public services. Integrating industry-specific knowledge with other open data, and applying advanced analytics to this combined pool of data, can create knowledge about customer preferences. This knowledge can assist in creating new services and products, and may avoid less popular features.

However, open data with limitless opportunities for societal benefits comes with its issues. The government, in its role as an open-data champion, needs to create policies that give confirmation and confidence to agencies that their data is safe and legally protected, and that only data mutually beneficial to the companies will be shared. For example, Yale University has introduced a project for pharmaceutical companies to safely publish their research on clinical trials. Those people who want to know more about this must submit an application, agree to use the data responsibly, and share their findings. If the data is wanted only for business purposes, permission is not granted. Thus, researchers use this data to help their investigation and contribute to overall knowledge. This collaborative effort can increase scientific knowledge by one company utilising efforts created by another.

Another aspect of sharing data is regulating the standards and speed of this “liquid” data so companies can share it without unnecessary delays and obstructions. Moreover, it should have a format that systems can use readily. For example, most companies now require their banking organisation to share transaction details above a threshold to check on money-laundering or tax-evasion activities.

Cloud and Big Data, Social Media

The collaborative framework will provide the government with guidelines to define information management of the large volume of data generated through social media and big data, and reduce the need for duplication of processing and storage of the same data collected from a number of smart-cities devices (Tadjeddine & Lundqvist, 2016) The data revolution will transform how the public sector services citizens, and enable better policies, services, and operations that are more productive. The reasons this will materialise shortly are twofold.

First, the already-low cost of computing power continues to decline, as do costs of data transportation, storage, and analysis. Analytic innovations such as Artificial Intelligence (AI) is simulating human intelligence by machine by using algorithms and other programming techniques. machine learning, and visualisation tools have made it possible to extract insights from very large datasets.

Second, data volumes have increased exponentially. Digital devices have become very popular, and new sources of data produce more and more of it for use and analysis. With the "Internet of Things," interconnected devices in use are expected to increase to 50 billion by 2020. Many of those devices are in smart-city programs, such as cameras and sensors in public areas. By 2020, smart-city usage in European cities will generate 100 e-bytes of data per day—four times more than the global data generated daily from all uses in 2015.

The breadth and diversity of this data can yield some critical insights, For example, the quality of police services improved with use of social media like Twitter to monitor public sentiment. More than four tweets from known gang members within a short span of time could raise concern and warn of potential criminal activity. Similar monitoring of potential terrorist activity or growing radicalism in a certain population could also occur.

Peer-to-Peer

Big and smart data requires smart technologies and smart capabilities to process it.

Peer-to-peer (P2P) networking is a distributed, decentralised application or database architecture in which peers form a network of nodes. The model is based on parallel computing, sharing the workload between peers that have equal rights. Because the load is divided, rapid sharing of voluminous amounts of data between nodes can occur. Sensitive data is shared securely, and any changes to the data are also confirmed by more than one peer to reduce the element of fraud. Authority for new members (ports) to join in comes through group voting by peers who are able to provide secure routing of network traffic.

The P2P interfaces should use information services to exchange information. The owners and contributors of the information must be defined. The P2P mechanism will provide real-time information between departments and agencies. The government information management may not be centralised, but an effective P2P framework will assist in seamless smart-government services accessing information from multiple departments or agencies. In a truly collaborative way, peers can bring in unique resources and capabilities, and accomplish tasks that could not have been done by individual peers, but have benefits for all. This peer-to-peer model has become popular due to its capacity to share a huge amount of resources among millions of users, where each peer can be a consumer or a provider. The Napster application is a good example, where music files can be shared across many grids and users.

Another example of peer-to-peer use in government is Seoul. Seoul has become congested through speedy growth followed by an economic downturn. The government came up with a neat solution: sharing their private physical spaces with other people (e.g., Airbnb-style housing, library spaces, gardens, parking spaces, goods sharing, and children's-clothes sharing). A shareHub where one can find all that can be shared in Seoul has become popular and provides benefits to all parties. By June 2014, $450,000 had been invested in 27 projects of Airbnb-style homesharing, parking-space sharing, and children's-clothing sharing. These projects resulted in 359 shared parking lots; a 68% increase in homestays; and children's clothing shared from 18,000 to 40,000 items as described by Seoul city model. Thus, by making the data available, new and innovative services are offered to the citizen. The government had to help set this up as a private-public network. Schools were set up to teach interested citizens how this model works and other required information. The housing issue has helped the older generation to become less isolated by renting out rooms to the younger generation, which has also led to a good intergenerational connection.

Of course this sharing comes with its own challenges. Regulations must be updated relating to laws on house sharing, insurance, and other issues that arise from sharing resources. However, there is a way forward for this, as the government gets insurance providers to propose solutions.

Video, Image, Sound

Current digital technology trends highlight how citizens are increasingly "living" online, and using public forums on the go to post opinions, provide personal information, and share content. The quick pace of adoption raises questions about how much privacy users can expect when using the Internet, and which laws govern freedom of expression of provocative content. Napster is good example of sharing music files across mobile devices, increasingly becoming the tools of choice for accessing the Internet, and amplifying security and privacy concerns. How best to prosecute those who infringe on others' intellectual property rights also remains a top concern for governments, businesses, and citizens.

Geospatial Information System (GIS) Data Framework

A Geospatial Information System (GIS) is a mapping system that allows users to query, search, analyse, understand, and present information geographically. Each department or agency could overlay relevant information, using common GIS data to assist in sharing information within government departments and with citizens. When governments fail, consequences can be severe. GIS systems can help alleviate this stress in many situations. For example, in major emergencies such as fires or floods, emergency services like ambulance, fire brigades, police, and social-service providers can overlay the location of all these services, and use geospatial analytics to point out the safest places for shelters for concerned citizens, all done in real time.

This information could enhance GIS capability with an enterprise-wide use along with Business Intelligence and Analytics capabilities. The GIS infrastructure across departments of the government should provide common services to its departments for location-based asset tracking, to equip decision makers to analyse and visualise the influence of geography on behaviours, activities, and processes. The GIS should deliver location-based intelligence and information to members in the field; and support data-driven decision making at strategic, operational, and tactical levels. To find the best places to put new hospitals, police centres, and community centres, information on local population, ethnic composition, economic profile, and other health clinics available in the area can help guide the decision. GIS will assist service planning by mapping areas of interest and enabling analysis of historical trend data on a geospatial basis.

INFORMATION MANAGEMENT FRAMEWORK

The objective of an information management framework (IMF) must be to provide context-based, secured, and correct information for the right person, in a usable format and at the right time. As depicted by Figure 3. IMF framework establishes rules, processes, standards, and implementation tools to manage information and data IMF must ensure users are presented with complete, valid, consistent, timely, and accurate information. This information should be fit for its intended use in planning, operations, and decision making. The IMF must ensure availability of accurate and appropriate information to assist with strategic planning and resource allocation that will reduce administrative burden across the organisation, resulting in less duplicate data entry, and easier access to crucial information. The IMF must ensure appropriate structures are in place to support informed decisions concerning information matters, including the ability to measure improvements in information quality and demonstrated benefit to the department.

Figure 3. Information management framework

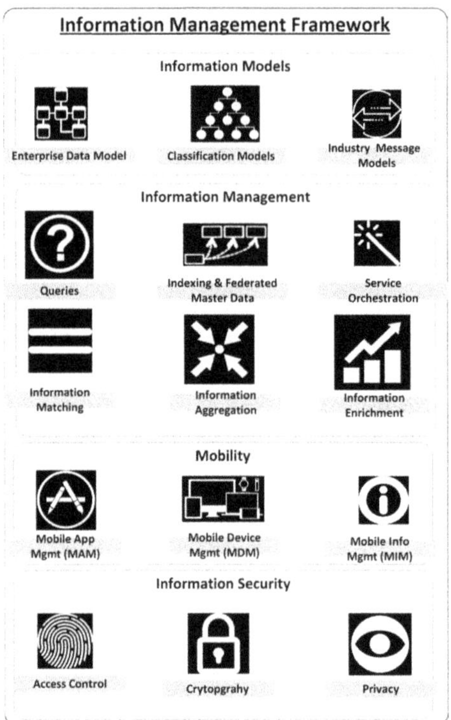

Information Security

Shareable data comes with the responsibility of ensuring privacy in transmission and use. Only those authorised to use the data should be able to see it. To manage that, CEAF will need to process information with varying degrees of security and privacy requirements. Centralised security policies and a business-rule engine will feed the information onto the framework. Security policies and business rules should be applied depending on whether information is internal or external.

Incoming information must create required keys, and categorize data security based on business rules. In the case of outgoing data, the framework must apply security profiles and only allow the user access to data according to role-based security needs.

Information Management

Successful implementation of CEAF will require centralised information distributions (publish and subscribe), information sharing, reporting, and analytic capabilities. Distribution of information to systems in an acceptable format is important, and will require centralised mapping of the key and information exchange.

A CEAF can also help ameliorate the following issues when collaborations incorporate emerging technologies:

- **Trust:** Each organisation will need to deposit information, based on quality parameters, which organisations can trust. The organisation also must comply with the withdrawal rules. Organisational responsibilities and data ownership will be required, along with effective and efficient data governance, discussed in Chapter 5.
- **Timelines:** It will be important to deposit information promptly for currency of the data. This could be achieved by defining some information services. The Service Oriented Architecture (SOA) framework will assist information owners in publishing information in a timely manner, and the subscribers in accessing current information. In government contexts, currency of information is critical, especially in health and law-enforcement areas.
- **Delivery of Information:** Delivery of information in the format consumable by the subscribing organisations is important. If the

information needs multiple translations before it is in a usable format, organisations will be reluctant to adopt this change. Proper delivery will necessitate a standard corporate data model such as NIEM (National Information Exchange Model). NIEM is a common vocabulary that enables efficient information exchange across diverse public and private organizations. NIEM connects communities of people who share a common need to exchange information in order to advance their mission (NIEM 2014) or ISO standard. Many government departments create standard format and data exchange methods. CEAF participating divisions and departments should adopt or agree on one of these standards. Data exchange could become an endless debate on the definition and differences for common entities. Hence, it is advisable to adopt the terminology closer to the meaning, which can be refined over time with CEAF maturity.

- **Cost and Resources Required for Establishing the CEAF Platforms:** Implementation of CEAF must consider cost and benefit of the approach. The cost of developing government-wide services will be less than accumulated costs of individual services. The funding structure will need to define these projects as foundation projects, and it should be assessed by its lifetime benefits to the agency developing it, and also to users of these services. The government could decide on a user-based cost allocation for the maintenance of the services, or set up a centre of excellence for various capabilities. These projects need to be managed in their infancy, and monitored to avoid costs that are prohibitively expensive; otherwise, organisations will revert to old ways of developing systems. Prioritisation of the services should not be based on the size or influence of the agency, but rather on citizens' needs, and prioritised and accepted across all government agencies.
- **Legislative and Contractual Framework:** Organisations will need to develop a framework to briefly define the contracts required for information sharing. This requires the right authority to share information and to understand legislative requirements. Government information needs to be secured, with context-based access and exchange. The legal framework should define what information could be shared to avoid any future legal claims and compensation.
- **Security:** E-government makes it easy to access and publish information. However, if not managed properly, the discretionary information supplied can breach a citizen's right to privacy. The transparency of decision rules and processes of the government must

be balanced with the right of the citizens to protect their own personal data. The CEAF should offer secure and contextual information to requesters. Security and transparency must be built into the design of the CEAF. The level of security and the kind of information being transferred depends on the culture and internal government structure of the country. However, public sentiment regarding openness of dealings and government decisions should be balanced with protecting private lives. Legal framework consists of the country's laws, regulations, and international treaty commitments. As suggested by various governments. Well-defined security and privacy of data is required in environments where on-premises, private-cloud, and third-party public-cloud services are used, with coordination between layers. The secure vaults layer must service all departmental needs, and should be agile enough to provide information depending on the context, without compromising information security. The government faces a wave of information collected from various public and private sources such as CCTV or social media. The classification of information must occur in real time. For example, a CCTV recording of the street could be unclassified; but if this information is required for any law-enforcement use such as riots or any criminal processing, then the information should be converted to another classification and shared accordingly.

- **Common Taxonomy:** Creation of a common language and taxonomy of architectures and solutions for the organisation and sharing interagency may require extensive consultation. The absence of common naming may have created data entities with different names, making consolidation of this information difficult, and requiring complex matching of names and a common language.
- **Creation of Enterprise Information Management Framework across All Departments of the Organisation:** The enterprise information-management framework will require creation, exchange, and governance of departmental and shared information across agencies and divisions. The information-management framework should define common rules of information exchange.
- **Alignment:** Ongoing alignment of data to the needs of citizens requires information augmentation rules to be defined, in order to keep the information real time.
- **Classification of Data:** Separation of data categories (structured and unstructured; transactional and analytical) is required to exchange and store this information securely. The enterprise digital asset

management systems (DAMS), if not already existing, must be planned and implemented. The DAMS must consist of services where information is managed (stored, searched, and accessed) according to its classification, type, and expected life. The information storage could use Clouds, in-house high-speed devices, or low-cost devices based on information classification and context.

- **Processes:** Having well-organised and well-documented processes for enhancement of data quality will be required. The information quality must be enhanced progressively. For example, if data is stored in multiple systems, then every time information is accessed, the information services should create a data-linkage key. This will assist the information services in improving performance by using the data-linkage keys as the first point of search, and updating the data linkages for new access.
- **Integration:** Integration between systems using an information services framework improves when the framework has secure and clear rules about what data should be shared, and in which format. It should provide timely and high-quality information. The information services should reflect the cost-benefits of data storage and usage. The framework over time should break down data silos and bring them together dynamically, to satisfy analytical requirements. The decision to use peer-to-peer or centralised information access should be based on the information volume and response time expected. In the case of centralised search, all the data must be available in a central location. This will create issues of volume of data transfer, currency of data, and data ownership (i.e., who owns the data after it is been deposited in a centralised location).

Peer-to-Peer computing could assist in federated search, where agencies may only need to provide metadata, to reduce the volume of data and increase the currency of information. The infrastructure is distributed so macroservices can run in parallel (in different jurisdictions), and information-aggregation technology could reduce the need for processing a large volume of data. The agencies will be comfortable with the information ownerships when they have up-to-date logs.

Establishing Good Governance, Risks, and Compliance

Information should be in a secure vault applied organisationally, and satisfy other legislative security requirements before it is exposed to any internal or external users. The secure vault will be temporary data storage that will also create the necessary keys for distribution from the accepted input. This will also enable creation of the required indexing for analytics. In turn, this will help to create keys for new data needs in services where each service must return system keys from owner systems, a requirement in order to have the flexibility to expand for future analytics

Smart Government adoptions require the organisation to plan enterprise-wide information-led services, or *Information Services*. This change is necessary for the information to flow from various agencies for organisational decision making and operations. For example, in Singapore, government is using mobile technology to help create intelligent transport services a number of frameworks are defined by governments across the globe (Singapore Goverment, 2015). An organisation using social-media data to decide on service design will require seamless information flow across the organisation. Starting with a list of challenges in information management in the age of Big Data, need has arisen for an architecture that will enable Collaborative Business Intelligence. The CEAF meets the needs of an ongoing industry-wide move toward centralisation of information. This is primarily due to the nature of current information, which requires strong collaboration and, in turn, architectural changes for a complete enterprise-view realignment to utilise existing investments by the organisations in infrastructure and service-oriented architecture. Changes must be implemented for the following key components.

- Information becomes knowledge when it is presented to the user, depending on need and context. While this framework can change, in many cases individual organisations can benefit through collaboration from the knowledge of each other's technologies and processes. For example, in a recent major "sticky accelerator" problem at Toyota, one could argue that collaborative intelligence could both help other car manufacturers learn from the knowledge gained in solving this problem, and help Toyota learn from others to avoid other potential problems in the future. Collaboration not only creates a tremendous opportunity in the manufacturing sector, but also in utility and service companies. For example, the call-centre context for the customer will change, depending upon the customer's request, and product and service details. Resolution of various customer requests might require a different knowledge base. In the case of a customer calling to report a problem with a product, the product's problem and resolution databases could be combined, and that knowledge could help resolve the issue.

- Business Intelligence (BI) provides insights into organisational capabilities, and bridges the gap between the vision of the organisation and its execution strategies. This enhances customer insights, and provides a better customer experience, as well as innovative products and services designed for target-customer segments. Such business intelligence has tremendous potential for application in the modern business world
- Collaborative Intelligence (CI) exists where all of the factors described so far are put to use for collaborative purposes. CI ensures that the business intelligence that is not part of organisational differentiation capabilities is shared with other organisations, reducing the need for each organisation to "reinvent the wheel." For example, mobile Web services can enable dynamic creation of intelligence based on the context of the user, and that enables personalised service to enhance customer experience (Tiwary & Unhelkar, 2011). When applied to handling environmental issues, CI is also described as Environmental Intelligence.

INFORMATION SHARING FRAMEWORK

Common Information Translation and Loading Framework

The Figure 4 depicts adopting information management from multiple sources requires an information translation and loading framework, because legacy data is still struggling with information connectivity between systems. The CEAF still requires legacy information to flow within and outside of the organisation for decision making. This information must be consistently translated into a consumable format for the distribution, necessitating creation of adequate indexing for the future analytics and searching. The security of information will be loaded in the secure vault before distribution, based on security profiles and business rules.

Figure 4. Information sharing framework

The intelligent theme builds on the way in which data-science and programming approaches are evolving to include Artificial Intelligence (AI) and advanced machine learning. This is enabling the creation of intelligent physical and software-based systems programmed to learn and adapt to the changed situation, rather than programmed only for a finite set of prescribed actions. AI and machine-learning capabilities are seeping into virtually every technology, and represent a major battleground for technology providers over the next five years.

Predictive Analytics

Predictive analytics signifies looking at data and its patterns, using machine-learning capabilities, and predicting a particular outcome of an event, based on the likelihood of its occurring—an event that has a certain chance of happening.

Across all levels of government are petabytes of structured and unstructured data collected, stored, and analysed from different agencies—for example, tax returns, unemployment claims, and hospital data. This information can be synthesised and used with other data to improve estimates, forecasts, and efficiency, and even to create new services. It can help set up an e-government that can deliver on the citizen's expectations, and provide services through a user-friendly system.

However, it is easy to lose one's way in complex data and among various techniques of deriving value from data. Very often, due to the complexity of predictive analytics, the CEO and other senior leaders can make the mistake of leaving it to the professionals. But this analysis should be directed and governed by senior managers to get useful and meaningful results.

Organisations must understand what insights they need in order to make good strategic and operational decisions. To get the right answers, the right questions must be asked of the data analysts. These questions arise from the formulated strategy, and the challenges of achieving that strategy form the questions for the analysts.

For instance, the strategy for the government could be to "reduce youth unemployment," or "improve the quality of life of our elderly citizens." To combat unemployment, the CEO needs to know the reasons youth are unemployed. It could be their education, frame of mind, job opportunities, and/or their family or social strata. They will need to know how many youth have been unemployed, where and for how long. Unemployment also calls for a deep dive into education, in this case a look at the student's education journey—explanations for drop outs and identifying the early signals so they can be diverted earlier on. There could also be a need to study and compare teachers' performance in schools. Perhaps young people need to be taught more vocational skills? If so, which would be needed, and where geographically? Would there be an excited take up of the new skills offered, or would more incentives be needed?

All these questions must be answered to get a whole picture of the issue. The involvement of senior managers throughout this journey is essential to keeping the direction of the analysis on its preferred path. Similarly, for the elderly, the managers need to know what the senior citizens need and where the gaps in those services exist. It would also help to know what other countries are doing to help their youth and the elderly to have good quality of life, to learn from other countries' experiences, and to build on them using local knowledge. For the elderly, some surveys can be taken to see if more senior citizen centres should be opened in certain localities, and if more helpers are needed to help the elderly at home and outside. There might be a possibility of getting the youth involved in looking after the aged, and gainfully employed for betterment of society.

Thus the strategy has to be translated into many clear questions, with each question addressed separately by the analysts. The results can be put together to formulate the line of action.

Financial constraints of implementation and planning will also decide the course of action to be taken to achieve the goal. But strategy will steer the path. All these insights help formulate a solution for reaching the desired goal. Thus, individual reasoning, logical thinking, machine-driven analysis, group surveys, and other means to arrive at valid answers, drive data analytics. No analysis of value is done on data. Adding value to decisions requires common sense, a sense of the happenings around us, and historical lessons, to name a few factors that help decide on the course/path to be taken to get to the next level.

Analytics deployment needs a team with many skills to get the results right. In the case discussed above, the team should have the following components.

- Data scientists should have the right technical skills and tools to analyse the data.
- Deployment strategy should be aimed at adoption and acceptance of the change. Experienced employees who have been working with the youth and the elderly in the society can help formulate the right strategy for implementation.
- Translators can link the strategy formulators' ideas to the technical people who work with machines. People who have business and systems knowledge would be required here.

This will mean that data from education, family economic and educational data, and police records all must be linked and aggregated. The data points must be comparable, and applications built that can put all the relevant data together. Solutions are always on the repeated cycle of implementing a proposed solution, analysing lessons from the implementation, and applying the lessons to the next phase of solution. Thus, application of analytics is a cyclic process of getting answers from data (internally collected data and external factors such as social media, economic factors, and global conditions), applying the best-suited solution (using experience and historical lessons), and gathering new data from this solution to help in the next phase of learning (Tadjeddine & Lundqvist, 2016).

Figure 5. Cyclic learning helps build knowledge

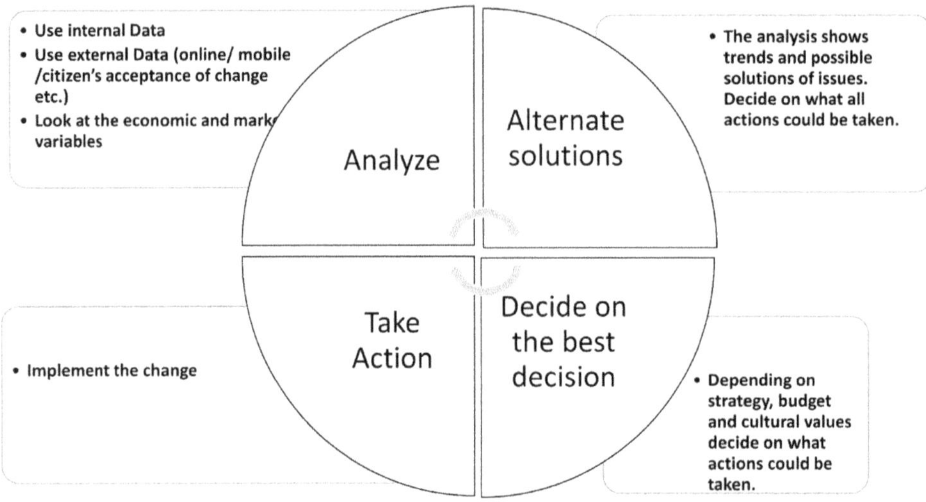

Communication between citizens and government can be improved through active involvement of the citizens. If interaction is easier and smoother and more efficient, then better relationships result (Harris & Mehrotra, 2014).

The Figure 5 depicts several sectoral views in a whole-of-government approach to what citizens would need for their lifetime. These analytic services can be outsourced to specialist companies who have enough experience to deal with this kind of analysis. For example, citizen digital identification could be done by the agency that will have information about most of its citizens, and augment its data with that from other agencies. Many countries have invested heavily in creating citizen-unique identifications that could be used in their digital identifications. For example, in Mumbai, India, property transfers now use biometrics online to uniquely and quickly identify a person.

Self-Service Reporting

Some business users like to explore and understand data on their own before they decide to take a particular action. Customers also like to see their transactions, profile, and company activities. By automating these and having tools that can help self-service management of these demands, the number of some requests made to call centres and back offices will drop. These data-discovery tools (for example, Tableau) allow for self-service BI, but with less IT involvement.

SERVICES LAYER

Collaboration requires moving away from assessing only internal data on the organisation's performance, to strategising by incorporating external data (big data, including social and mobile media in various formats) relevant to organisational operations. Collaboration, rather than competition at any cost, can be viewed as a valid business strategy. The breathtaking rapidity of growth in communications, storage, and analytics leads to the strategic viewpoint that in a shrunken world, collaboration is a much better way of competing than direct competition. That is also an intelligent way of looking at the business world. Business Intelligence (BI) can be understood as the creative use of data and information by the organisation, in a way that results in new bodies of knowledge that can also be applied in practice. Collaborative Intelligence (CI) takes BI to the next level, where intelligence is synergised within and across multiple organisations, to produce actionable value for the collaborators. This is the key to success in big data–driven business strategies. Such CI is not limited to a single organisation. In fact, practical CI would render traditional organisational boundaries highly porous. Thus, collaboration is a fundamental shift in business values, needs, and strategies (Sherringham & Unhelkar, 2010).

Knowledge (i.e., correlating information) provides insights to users who can use it in an appropriate way. Intelligence takes knowledge to further abstraction and, at the same time, provides actionable insights regarding predictive behaviour. For example, in the medical industry, insurance organisations can correlate hospital admissions with income levels, and thereby bring about a potential reduction in insurance costs through appropriate distributions of the client base. As another example, an intelligent airline can not only correlate passenger traffic with weather information, but also produce personalised schedules for passengers, depending on their travel purpose (e.g., family visit, business visit, or medical emergency). Finally, consider a patient in a hospital. He is interested in the end-to-end patient flow that handles his requirements from entering the hospital to being diagnosed, investigated, treated, and discharged. Such a holistic process requires collaboration among numerous organisations and agencies, such as the hospital administration, the medical and surgical staff, the pathology laboratories, the pharmacies that disburse medications, the insurance companies that provide the medical coverage, transportation agencies such as the ambulance services, and much more. The patient is not interested in the interconnections among these various agencies,

Figure 6. Service layer framework

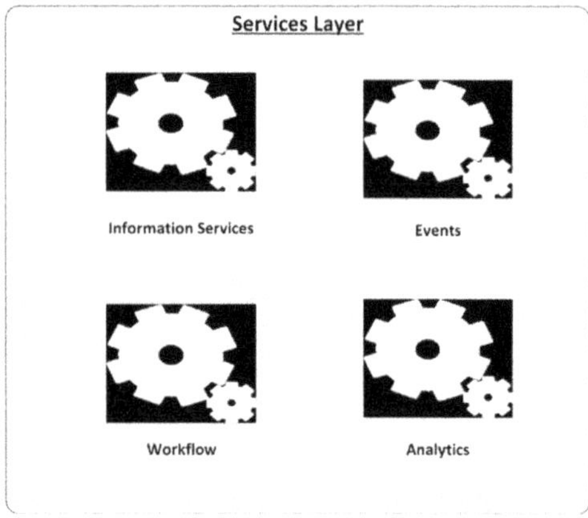

but only in the result. These scenarios depict the creative and dynamic use of data, information, and knowledge, taken from varied sources making a citizen's life better.

An information services platform as depicted in Figure 6 provides services such as:

- **Consolidation:** Depending on the information requested, data is extracted from various sources and constructed into reports. This consolidation of data can be scheduled based on the business rules, and frequency and type of requests. For example, all sales departments will need information at two levels: by each product and by a summary at various aggregation levels. Defining "object-relational" rules for the itemised data could consolidate the summary information (Stonebraker, 1997). Weekly, monthly, and yearly summary data types for products could be defined within the database, making business queries simpler and quicker.
- **Articulation:** Service provides the data translation, based on organisational business rules. This could be a service that supplies on demand and as part of some request for data or service. This articulation of services could be scheduled regularly, depending on the reporting requirements, and will translate the data into information.
- **Personalisation:** Items and their information levels and details have a different context in each department. Marketing and sales will look at the same data, but marketing might want to see the sales on the campaigns published by the company, whereas sales might want to

look at the weekly sales by stores. Personalising the reports will make them user-friendly and readily usable and useful.

- **Shared Services:** A shared services library will provide each organisation with a set of services that will be used for collaborative-intelligence services. The current use of cloud computing in association with Web services will be required.

An information services framework will provide a set of generic services definition and usage. Either of the organisations or a software vendor provider could develop these services. The BI will move towards predictive analytics

Timely, Available, Contextualised Systems

Personalised and relevant information exchange improves organisations' relationships with customers and constituents. IT technicians who deploy customer-centric communications, either directly or on the Web can enrich the customer's experience as well as their loyalty and brand awareness.

Customer communications management (CCM) is now changing its approach from delivering a generic message to managing the customer relationship by delivering relevant and timely communications. These communications could occur by way of multiple channels (such as Web, email, SMS, and print), and devices including laptops, phones, and tablets. Of course, this dynamic and interactive model is increasing the complexity of needed solutions and skill sets. The messaging can take the context of what the customer is doing online (on mobile), and his possible life-stage needs, keeping in mind any preferences he has shown historically to push messages. This requires keeping offline and digital information about the customer readily available and able to be synthesised in any of the devices from which the customer might want to connect. This experience can deliver an engaging relationship based on customer understanding. Tool selection for such management should be able to process pertinent customer information readily. If a customer must get a regulatory letter in the mail, it should be available online as well, and the customer should be able to look for it and read it online. Those technologies should enable such self-service data. Web Content Management (WCM is a software system that provides tools to create and manage website content easily) solutions and portals are an increasingly popular choice among companies. Key ingredients for creating new and more interactive experiences include:

- Data Quality and Analysis to assess customer engagement by analysing clicks made, pages left, pages followed through, log files, and other behaviours.
- Access and delivery of message across all channels and within a channel.
- Personalised, relevant, and contextual customer communications.
- Digital data considered part of the asset.
- Data available on different devices and technological platforms.

Government departments are sharing their business intelligence for the win-win outcome without compromising their market position and differentiation. Such collective business intelligence was evident during the recent global financial crisis, as various governments coordinated the response across multiple cross-sections of different industries (Goel, Tiwary Schmidt, 2010). This is achieved by correlating seemingly unrelated pieces of information that may reside in a silo. For example, a hospital may have information on a group of patients suffering from a certain type of cancer; an apparently unrelated piece of information hidden away elsewhere may come from, say, their residential postcode (i.e., area where they live). Correlating these two types of information may provide insight into the nature of that geographical area and its potential relationship to the cause of cancer.

From a technology perspective, collaborations require the ability to ask business the right questions; and for the business to be able to sensibly concur with or deny the emanating value.

CORPORATE APPLICATIONS

Suite Applications

Technological progress for in-memory computing has made big data easier to handle. In this kind of memory, storage of information is in RAM of dedicated servers. Speeding up retrieval of information, as traditional databases make the input/output of information slower, helps corporations analyse massive volumes of data and perform operations 10,000 times faster than standard disk data. With the advances in technology, memory prices have been dropping as well, which makes in-memory very affordable.

Along with this, the emergence of corporate planning and modelling CPM solutions has enabled strategists to improve corporation budgeting and

Figure 7. Corporate applications

planning capabilities radically. This is a business-driven and owned solution, its life cycle based on business capabilities.

These are specialist applications loosely coupled to create an agile architecture that responds to business needs quickly as depicted in Figure 7.

Cloud Applications

Microsoft's cloud computing on the Azure platform is the hybrid provider, building integration between existing on-premises IT assets and cloud resources

Years of cuts have left IT departments struggling to operate bi-modally—that is, innovation and running operational activities efficiently. However, with the advent of big data and new technologies on its way, CIOs must move away from focussing on cutting costs in the infrastructure, and look at improvements in the value chain, processes, and end-to-end transactions. Delivering innovation and new solutions should be the true mission.

Government CIOs should plan to ensure that the organisation obtains the necessary capabilities to deliver the digital government agenda as depicted in Figure 8. They must recognise their organisations' need for innovation and incorporate new technologies disrupting their organisations.

Figure 8. Cloud options

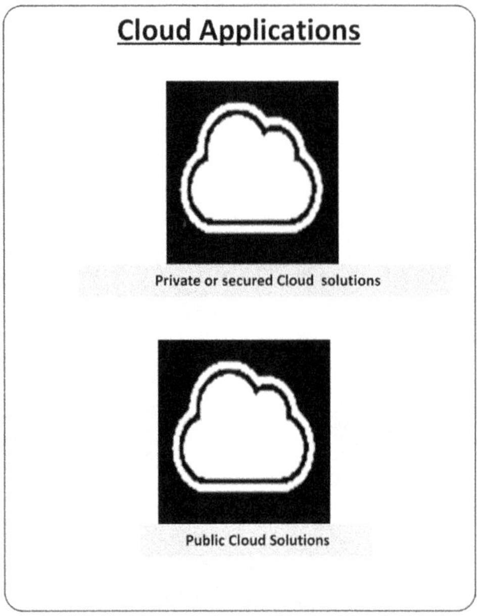

Infrastructure

The information services framework should support creation or use of either a private or public Cloud, with adequate security and authorisation to access stored information (Goel, Tiwary, & Schmidt, 2010). The Cloud should support information and services available to users, irrespective of its location (internal to the organisation or shared information from other companies).

The security framework will define what information the organisation will share, based on its sustainability rules. The information that differentiates the organisation will be secure from sharing.

Generic business rules will be based on the standards developed by the information entities, and on industry standards. They should be implemented in the organisation-wide application framework. For example, addresses in standard ISO 9000 format could be used to share and store location information. The standards need to be refined for collaborative information sharing.

Generic information translation rules will be developed to interpret the shared information. The need for translation should diminish over time if generic business rules are adopted for organisation-wide storage and use of data entities.

Figure 9. Infrastructure framework

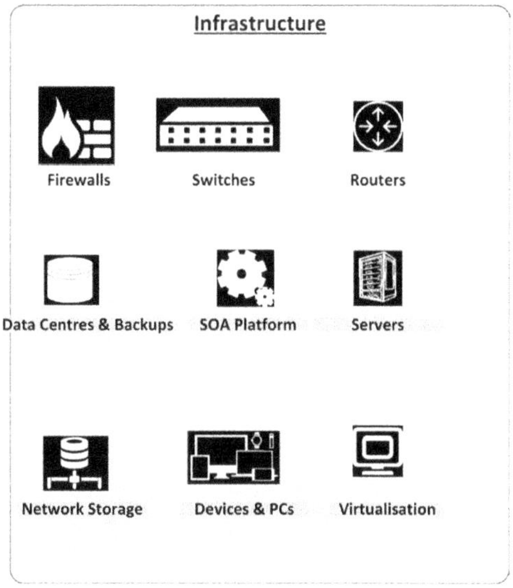

Other components of the information will maintain business rules, security policies, and quality criteria that must be applied to the information.

The information extraction platform will provide services to extract information from various data sources.

Figure 9 depicts systems are integrated for on-demand information access, based on services, and toolsets with enhanced capabilities. The integration should reduce the number of servers currently in use for business-intelligence activities.

Business processes for data cleansing, data quality, and security are defined and implemented, and thus provide the customer with "right information, on time" (Goel, Tiwary, & Schmidt, 2010).

Firewalls

The security of applications running on cloud services is of concern to citizens and IT professionals.

Some industries, such as healthcare, have highly confidential data, and their regulatory and legal requirements might not always be understood by cloud services, making the department noncompliant without its knowledge. Thus, it is more comfortable for data stewards to keep critical data within their firewalls.

Nowadays there are mature technologies and advanced hardware firewalls (for instance, crypto chips), which can allow varying levels of security for different products.

Switches

Many enterprise services cannot stop working without harmful consequences. As we digitize this world to one in which a citizen can expect to go online and perform almost all civic needs, we also need to ensure that networks can run continuously and give service in the shortest timeframe possible. There should be a way to scale networks up or down quickly without months of preparation. A distributed architecture helps prevent system delays due to hardware failure.

Switches can regulate traffic flow to any network address, and security and efficiency are thus maximised. They do not just retransmit every data packet to every port to which they are connected, which would reduce efficiency, but only to the device/hub that needs to receive it.

Such systems improve efficiency, security, speed of transmission, and stability of applications.

Routers

As public cloud computing is introduced to process information, it also adds processing overhead and degrades application response times. Videos and images are frequently transmitted across network layers, which can saturate Wide Area Networks (WAN). Applications like email and data backups are not response-time-sensitive, whereas some critical applications need a real-time response. Also, enterprises continue to demand improved performance of their applications, and thus enterprise-class routers can help enable this efficiency.

Data Centres and Backups

Applications that interact with customers and transactional data, and manage supply chains, are critical to the organisation, and must reside and be hosted in a secure environment. Data centres are not cheap to build and operate, and it is hard to know future requirements, especially in a fast-growing world.

Migrating applications to a cloud platform is an excellent way to limit data-centre capacity requirements.

Consolidation of data centres can help too, but usage is needed for an accurate estimate of infrastructure. Also, funds might be allocated to each agency separately and by project, making it difficult to determine the real cost of the data centre.

Servers

Companies operating in a digital world have applications that operate 24/7, and any server downtime can impact services negatively.

Digital data that resides on servers grows exponentially, and so would the need for extra servers. Cloud computing can help save costs for noncritical applications by improving automated capacity increase and decrease, easy server deployment, and balanced throughput.

Government agencies often have their servers, and staff to manage them. Consolidation, though complex, is a good way to reduce costs and keep the server load distribution and upkeep well balanced.

Network Storage

The amount of data has been growing rapidly, and with the advent of big data, petabytes of data accumulate in a matter of weeks, to the point where costs outstrip storage budgets and staff productivity. Management of storage is becoming a challenge.

Approaching storage needs rationally can overcome some of these costs and issues. Consideration of what data must be stored and segmentation of customers might help in deciding how much data to store in locations that are easy to access. For example, most bank customers might want to access only the last two months' data, and it might not be cost effective to store the last two years' data. Big organisations often store duplicate data in different teams. This duplication is wasteful and avoidable if some investigation and analysis occur on where and how it is used, and how best to transfer it quickly from a single storage point to a required site. Peer-to-peer servers are being used to transfer large amounts of data securely.

Data should be classified as critical or noncritical, and storage should be decided based on how critical it is. New storage devices are agile and, though expensive (e.g., Solid State Arrays), are nearly autonomous and easy to use.

Critical data can be kept on these devices, as well as data requiring real-time synchronised backup.

Adopting new technologies, such as solid-state, Cloud, HCIS, software-defined and open-source solutions, will support future infrastructure's improved performance, agility, user friendliness, and decreased operating costs. Managing and distributing storage of devices so common in government agencies is better supported, and these technologies are easier to scale upward as well.

Public Acceptance of Digital Government

Apart from implementing the necessary technical tools and know-how, the change management required for public acceptance of this move to smart government is extremely important. Certain barriers to using public services online might arise, which, if ignored, will make the implementation less smooth.

One such barrier is acceptance of private data being available online, even if it is secure. Big data creates new opportunities and has the potential to transform the way the public interacts with the government. It also enables collecting data on the individual's behaviour: what applications are used and for what purposes, what transactions are taking place, any suspicious behavior, and other services that might be required. At the same time, big data can be used to create an open and transparent government. But the public and the government must trust each other and believe that the collected data will be used for the benefit of improving civic life; and that if it must be published, the negative impact will be minimised. To develop this trust, government can provide information on:

- Government rules and citizen rights;
- Government decisions and actions;
- Monitoring government actions and expenditures;
- Government performance; and
- Government processes, like land records, applications for licenses, and status of tax payments.

Though the data has historically resided in hard-copy folders, trust must be maintained that it will only be used for the citizen's private purposes. Trust must be rebuilt and reconfirmed that "My Data" is only available to the citizen, and is probably more secure than ever before. Trust in e-government can be built through increased responsiveness to inquiries. Usability of the application, search facilities, and the technology also will impact on its popularity. Transparency and privacy are important societal and democratic values, required to inform citizens and let them participate in democratic processes. Practices in these areas are changing with the rise of new information-savvy generations and social media's role in information sharing. Although intuitively appealing, the concepts of transparency and privacy have many interpretations and are difficult to conceptualise, making their implementation difficult. Transparency and privacy should be conceptualised as complex, no dichotomous constructs interrelated with other factors. Only by conceptualising these values in this way can the nature and impact of on privacy and transparency be understood, and their levels balanced with security, safety, openness, and other socially desirable values.

Citizen ability to use the online applications and availability of computers and Internet may represent another barrier to acceptance. Many segments of a population (especially the older generation) still prefer in-person or phone-based conversation with a government representative. Dedicated offices must be set up, where they can walk in and someone can show them how to use the system, until they are comfortable with the application and their questions are answered. Government officials should be trained in government processes and applications, and able to respond clearly and succinctly so citizens can understand how to operate the system, and have faith that their

Figure 10. Information flow between citizen and offices

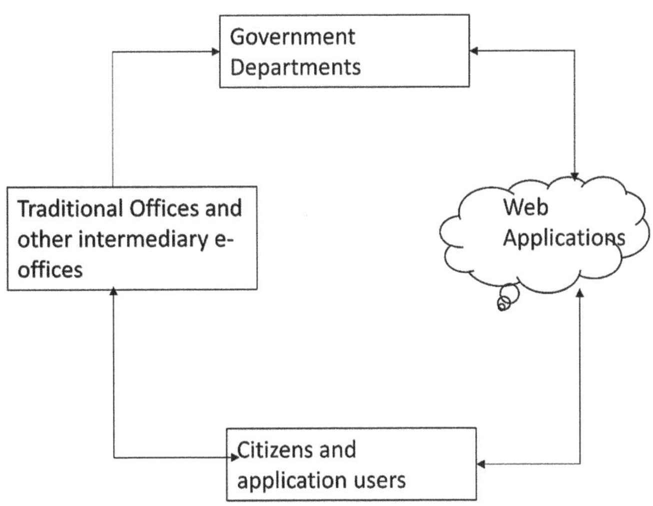

own information is going to be safe. There will always be a need for a few offices and government officials that actually do the work on behalf of the citizens (Adhaar, 2014) as shown in Figure 10.

REFERENCES

Australian Government. (2016). *Smart cities plan overview*. Retrieved from https://cities.dpmc.gov.au/smart-cities-plan

Australian Government Cloud Computing Policy. Version 3.0. (2014, October). Retrieved from http://www.finance.gov.au/sites/default/files/australian-government-cloud-computing-policy-3

Australian Government. (n.d.). Retrieved from https://www.access-info.org/transparency-and-privacy

Berlot, J., Jaeger, P., & Grimes, J. (2010, July). Using ICTs to create a culture of transparency. *Government Information Quarterly*, *27*(3), 264–271. doi:10.1016/j.giq.2010.03.001

Chui,, M., Anyika, J., & Kuiken, S. (2014, January). What executives should know about open data. *The McKinsey Quarterly*.

Goel, A., Tiwary, A., & Schmidt, H. (2010). Approaches and Initiatives to Green IT Strategy in Business. In B. Unhelkar (Ed.), *Handbook of Research on Green ICT: Technical, Methodological and Social Perspectives*. Hershey, PA: IGI Global.

Harris, J., & Mehrotra, V. (2014, Sep 16). Getting value from your data scientists. *Computer Weekly Digital*.

NIEM. (2014). Retrieved from https://www.niem.gov/

Seoul. (n.d.). *Sharing Seoul City Model*. Retrieved from http://www.shareable.net/blog/sharing-city-seoul-a-model-for-the-world

Sherringham, K., & Unhelkar, B. (2010a). Customer centric business strategy aligning business and IT. *Cutter Consortium Business-IT Strategies Executive Report, 13*(10).

Sherringham, K., & Unhelkar, B. (2010b). Achieving business benefits by implementing enterprise risk management. *Cutter Consortium Enterprise Risk Management and Governance Executive Report, 7*(3).

Singapore Government Regulations Licensing and Consultation. (n.d.). Retrieved from https://www.imda.gov.sg/regulations-licensing-and-consultations/consultations/consultation%20papers/2015/proposed-regulatory-framework-and-standards-for-its

Tadjeddine, K., & Lundqvist, M. (2016, Aug). *Policy in the data age: Data enablement for the common good.* Digital McKinsey.

Tiwary, A., & Unhelkar, B. (2011). Extending and Applying Business Intelligence and Customer Strategies for Green ICT. In B. Unhelkar (Ed.), Handbook of Research in Green ICT: Technical, Business and Social Perspectives. IGI Global.

ENDNOTE

1 *Publish and subscribe* is a term used in Service oriented Architecture (SOA), where Publish is list of information that is available to users of the services. Subscribers are the users of information who are authorised by the publisher to access the information.

Chapter 3
Adopting CEAF

ABSTRACT

The proposed CEAF will urge government departments at all levels to share information such as budgets, to allow for the creation of better solutions for the whole-of-government. Existing initiatives are currently limited to the procurement "economy of scale" level, or a superficial collaboration necessitated by an information exchange requirement within various departments of government. As envisaged in this work, the CEAF is defined as the link between government strategy and the corresponding capabilities and technology assets of the whole-of-government in action.

INTRODUCTION

The adoption of the collaborative enterprise architecture framework (CEAF) within a current government environment requires careful and focused planning. A big-bang approach, where government departments suddenly move from their current systems to new common systems, will not work. The change must be planned and implemented in an iterative approach, where there is an option to resolve a present pressing need without compromising on the future state of architecture. The CEAF provides a mechanism to optimise the use of legacy systems. This approach provides the mechanism to adopt a phased implementation of the CEAF. The CEAF should take a pragmatic approach, where the end state is defined, and many phased decisions are made to achieve it in a planned manner.

DOI: 10.4018/978-1-5225-2407-6.ch003

A political cycle of elections held within a government term drives its departments. Commitments made by the ruling party to its electorate during the elections drive its focus and direction.

The following criteria should be kept in mind when planning the adoption of CEAF:

- Legacy systems should be modified in a planned approach, as and when opportunity arises to do so.
- The initial adoption of the CEAF must be as a pilot with only a few data entities or systems involved in the beginning.
- The CEAF must be planned and implemented in an incremental format

ADOPTING COLLABORATIVE ENTERPRISE ARCHITECTURE FRAMEWORK

The adoption of the CEAF at the government level will require overall alignment of government and individual agencies or departments with the framework, which will also require government-wide enterprise architecture and a defined end state. For this initiative, the government must set up a business capability-based services framework. Business capabilities are the way in which enterprises combine resources, competencies, information, processes, and their environment, to deliver consistent services to citizens. They are used to describe what the government does, and what it will need to do differently in response to strategic challenges and opportunities. Thinking in terms of business capabilities is one of the ways organisations understand and express how they combine technologies and processes to deliver value. What makes business-capability modelling unique is its focus on what the business does in the present timeframe, and what must change so that the new Web-based technologies do not dismantle the working of the government, but allow it to make use of the opportunities inherent in these new technologies. The information-services development for such services will require two levels of decision making. At the whole-of-government level, the enterprise information services should be able to define the context and level of security required for service outcomes; on the individual-organisation level, the currency of information and source systems must be defined. In some cases, the information service may not be a pure service. It might provide data to the servicing layer. Figure 1 depicts an overall information-services framework. The enterprise-wide services may be provided entirely by a participating agency or department, or performed at the CEAF common-services level by aggregating the information from various sources. The services architecture must have the following components defined:

- **Information Clouds:** These should provide context-driven information services to both internal and external users. The services definition should be generic so that different departments can use it, and follow the enterprise data model for exchange of information.
- **Information Services:** Platforms should synthesise information collected from internal and external sources and apply business rules; check and clean quality of data; and apply security rules to personalise, articulate, and consolidate information services.
- **Collaborative Data Extract Services:** Information from data services will be extracted and converted to collaborative information services. This layer will encapsulate the legacy systems and should reduce the impact of legacy remediation on the information services. The coexistence of legacy systems with the new application will be a reality, and it is important to provide a mechanism for replacing the legacy systems in a planned approach, without affecting citizen services. Citizen Services can be defined as services requested by a citizen such as applying for building permit. Internally many multiple agencies collaborate to provide this service. This concept requires internal collaboration so the citizen does not have to contact multiple agencies.
- **Information Aggregation Services:** Data sources will assemble information required for the information services from various internal and external sources. Data sources are envisioned to include structured and unstructured information. Processing static information once and creating BI databases that will assist in expediting the performance of the service are recommended.
- **Infrastructure Services:** Infrastructure will consist of both legacy and modern components. The decision to interconnect agencies at the infrastructure level will require extensive consultation and security assessment, but will assist in building better collaborative information services.

Figure 1. Overall view of CEAF adoption

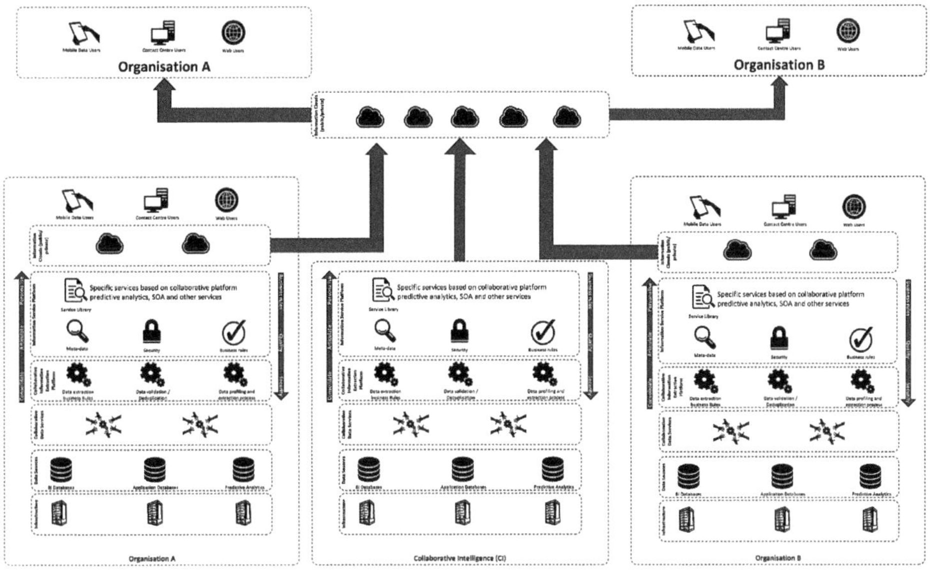

Amit Tiwary -Collaborative enterprise architecture framework©

The adoption of the CEAF will need to be organised as depicted in Figure 1. It will require identifying common services to be provided in response to all information requests. A Citizen Information request, such as passport extension, will require some common services. For example, any government interaction may require information from multiple agencies, such as vital statistics departments for verifying personal details, road and traffic departments for licenses or traffic offenses, and local government's areas for information on properties, to accumulate the complete information set. The adoption must be pragmatic and strategic. Participating agencies and departments will need to finalise some foundation pieces, such as the enterprise corporate data model and information services definition frameworks, to be able to provide this standard information. This will require creating a formal group for an enterprise architecture forum that will define government's services. It should define the information services that will be available, and information data sources that will be required. This services directory can then assess the current state of the services, and define a roadmap to achieving collaborative services.

Figure 2. Individual organisational view of the CEAF adoption

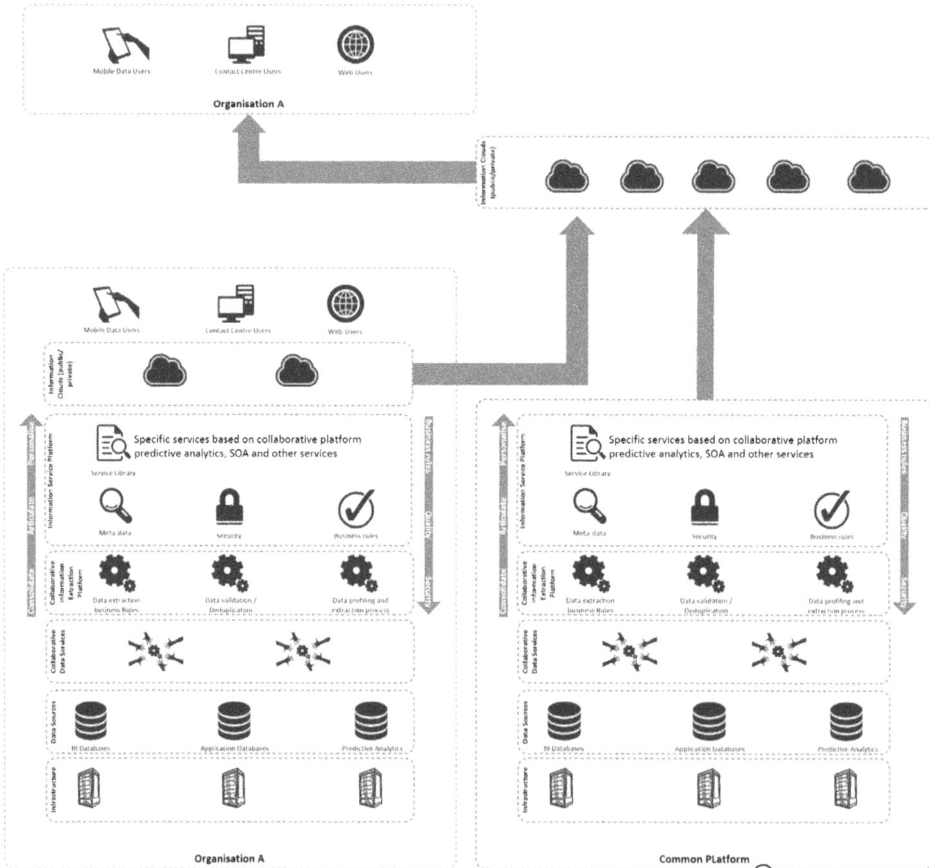

Amit Tiwary -Collaborative enterprise architecture framework©

The service directory should define the owners of the services. Participating departments and agencies could also adopt a similar structure internally. The framework could be an extension of the existing enterprise architecture framework with collaborative information services added. The individual agencies will agree to participate in collaborative services with predefined and mutually agreed-upon service levels. Figure 2 depicts the collaboration of information services. In some cases, the organisational constraints of the legacy systems will restrict the information services platforms. Here, individual organisation or government-wide infrastructure should be defined for the common services, as depicted in Figure 3.

As depicted in Figure 3, the common service should define, at an enterprise level, the current and expected use of this service across all government

Figure 3. Common services view of CEAF adoption

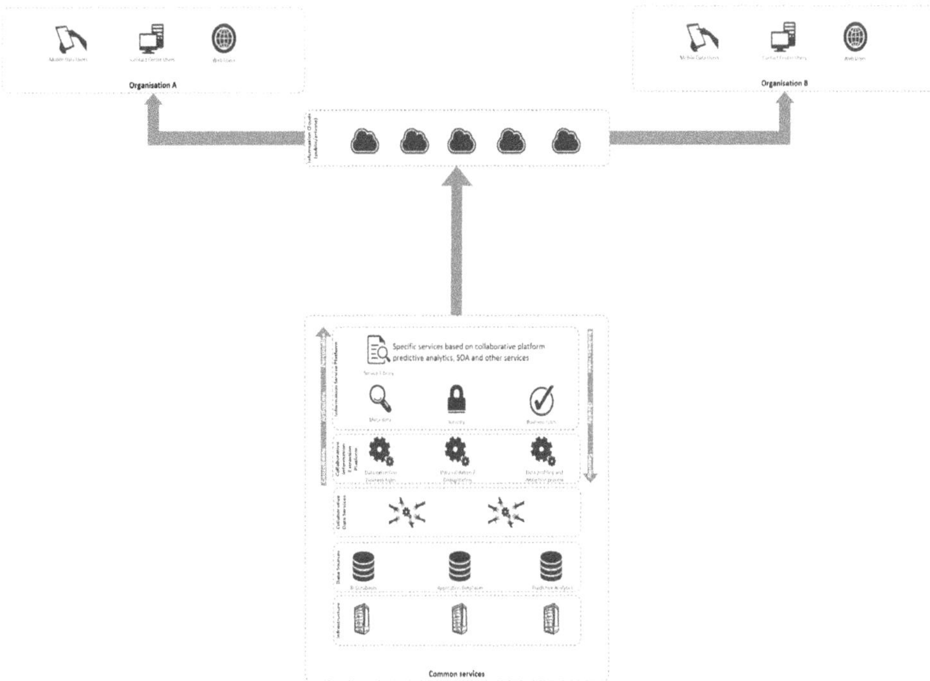

Amit Tiwary -Collaborative enterprise architecture framework©

departments. The services definition should allow for the information services to coexist with different versions of systems (new and legacy). It should optimise the information flow depending on users' needs. The government will need to define the common-services framework at the enterprise level, and should consider requirements from all large and small departments. The design should provide flexibility and agility to add or modify information needs over time, without major enhancements to the information services. The participation of all agencies and departments of the government must be promoted, and should be governed by the project investment committees. Once the enterprise information service is defined, any new investment requests from the individual departments must be examined to see if the current services can provide the required functionality. Chapter 5 discusses this kind of governance in more detail.

The user access system will need to be defined at an enterprise level, to provide access to departmental information across the whole-of-government. Identity and Access Management (IAM) is the combination of business processes and technology used to manage digital identities and access to

Figure 4. Reorganising users based on CEAF

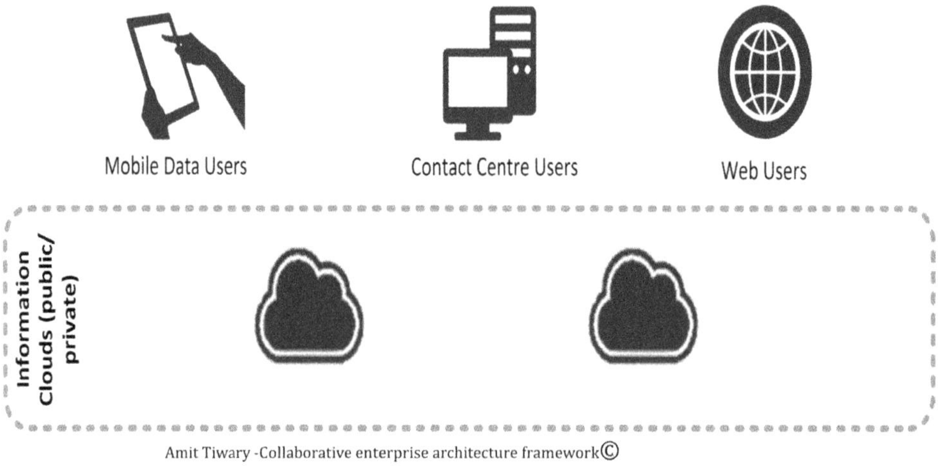

departmental applications, databases, and systems. IAM services provide controlled access to business data and technology services, based on an individual's role and responsibilities within the organisation. In many departments and agencies, IAM may still use manual processes to provide access to its users. The CEAF objectives are to provide seamless access to information, based on a user's roles and responsibilities. These services will require automation of IAM processes. Figure 4 depicts a way to create information cloud structure. Departmental services can provide information in a cloud Enterprise Data model framework. The information Cloud then applies security rules and provides information in context to the users. P2P networks can apply role-based security without the need to involve a central server-based authorisation approach. This model makes it faster to transfer huge volumes of data without compromising the security of the data (Park & Hwang, 2003).

The information services platform depicted in Figure 5 is an adaptation of the information collection and services framework. The information services platform provides the mechanism for collecting information based on the context and security level of the user. Business rules, quality of data, and security of data will decide the content of the information services. The services will consolidate, personalise, and present the information in a comprehensible manner. The services definition is more of an abstract concept. The implementation of these services could be a hybrid of a legacy data exchange system and adaptation of any enterprise services framework. The

Figure 5. Using information management framework

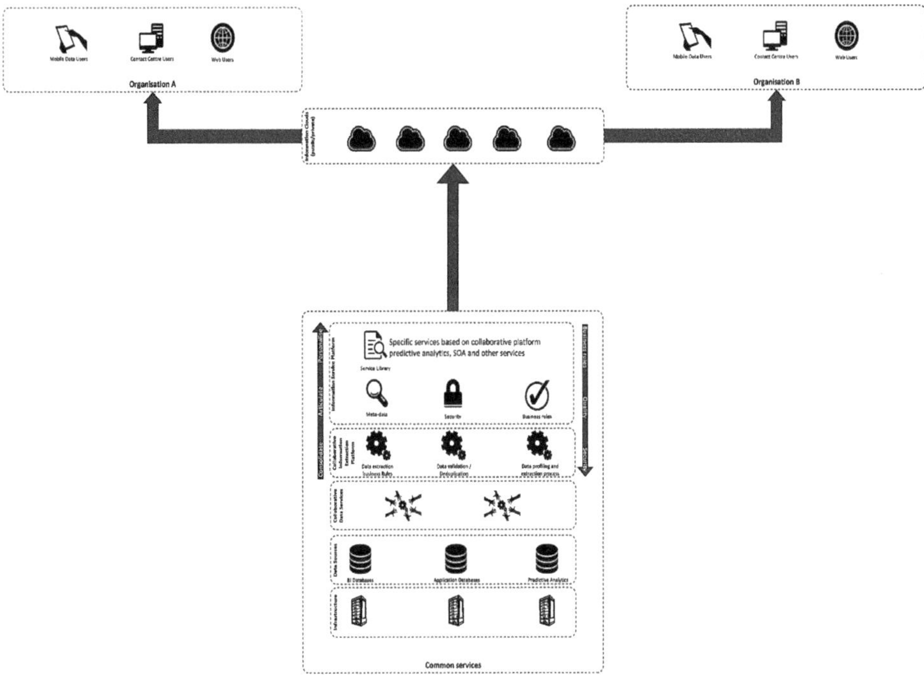

Amit Tiwary -Collaborative enterprise architecture framework©

CEAF adoption should identify services that will be required and developed at the enterprise level. The legacy data can still be processed and collected in information Clouds for reformatting, which will elevate the need of updating legacy systems or reformatting current information sources.

The information management framework depicted in Figure 6 should be utilised to develop information services, which in turn will define the data-extraction business rules. The organisation should initiate the adoption of a standard data model. In many cases, this should start with adopting the taxonomy of a standard data model. Full compliance with any standard data model, such as NIEM (National Information Exchange Model [NIEM], 2014) be planned in phases. The first phase should be the adoption of NIEM as an information reference architecture, where naming conventions and entity attributes are consistent with the NIEM model. This adoption will assist all participating agencies to adopt a common enterprise data model. The legacy systems data model may differ from the corporate data model. An attempt to change legacy systems to accommodate a new data model may be expensive, and have a limited life if the legacy systems are earmarked for replacement. In such cases, updating any of these data models is not recommended. The information management framework must be tasked with any data transformation and translation between legacy data models and the enterprise data model. The translation rules must be defined as part of the collaborative information extraction platform. This platform also could be used to incrementally eliminate duplication of data and build information linkage keys if no master data management systems (MDM) are in place. MDM is a method enables an enterprise to link all its critical data in one source or database. This source becomes the common reference point for all departments. These services should follow the information collection, articulation, and personalisation processes based on business rules, data quality,

Figure 6. Information services framework

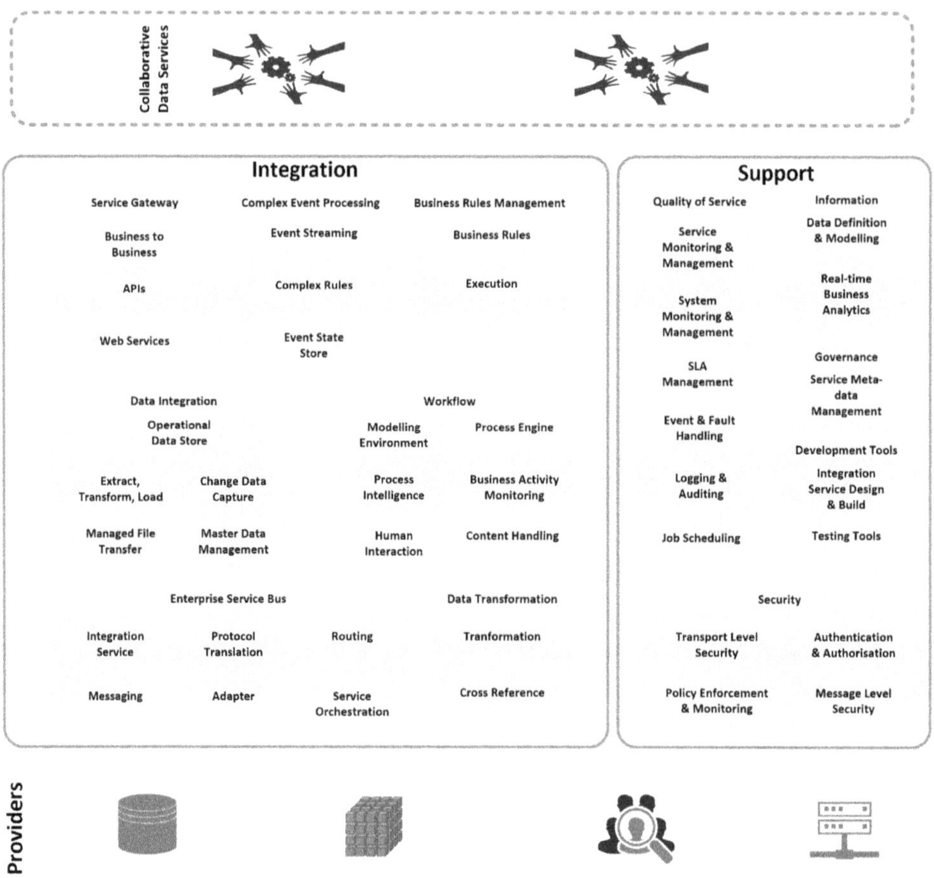

Amit Tiwary -Collaborative enterprise architecture framework©

Figure 7. Infrastructure framework

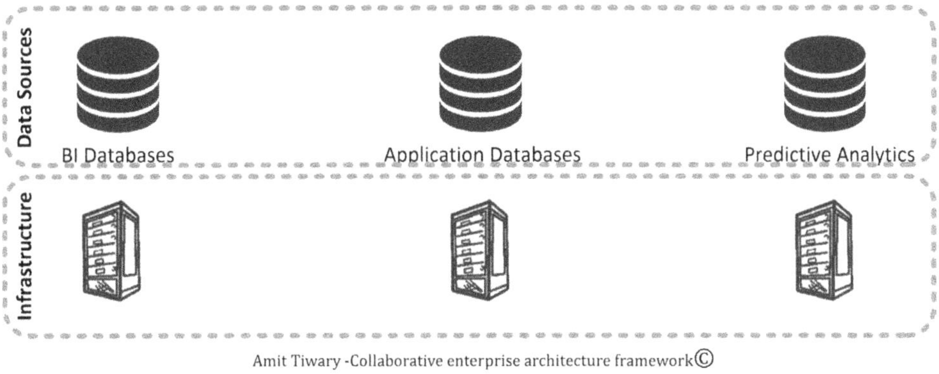

and security classification of the information. The information management framework should provide information services for both internal and external information, where applicable. The building of the information framework must occur in phases, and should avoid "boiling the ocean."

The infrastructure framework should define the required information in consumable format for the services, as shown in Figure 7. The information requirements and format translation assessment must be conducted to optimise the use of BI databases and predictive analytics in the information services. The schema of BI and predictive information databases should adopt the enterprise data model and simplify data exchanges. The infrastructure framework should be defined for modernisation of legacy applications, by encapsulating information within legacy systems so it can be used by information services.

CHANGES IN FUNDING CYCLE

The CEAF adoption will require the government to change its funding model and cycle. The projects must be defined at two levels

1. **Foundation Projects Funding:** At this level, the main components required to support specific business objectives for the next five to ten years are developed. These components are part of the initial roadmap/ foundation project for multi-use initiatives. These are designed for organisational requirements, but delivered with some key specific requirements. Requirements are documented as capabilities required

by the business to support specific business objectives. The design of these initiatives should include considerations for other projects and future capabilities required. This design may be costlier than specific projects, but benefits of these initiatives need to be calculated for overall program delivery, rather than a single project outcome.

2. **Agency-Based Services Development Funding:** The collaborative enterprise services need each participating agency to develop the structure and architecture that will enable it to provide supporting services. This funding is for the development of services of these agencies.

The governance process must allow for a project's proposal of service, based on the capabilities being built. The capability-building proposals must demonstrate the functionality proposed on both the agency level and the whole-of-government level. The governance process must be transparent and should identify the government priorities in building the capability of citizen services. The project-idea initiators should be accountable for the benefit that is claimed, which must be audited. In some cases, government funding for the foundation projects that is adequate and well planned will reduce the doubling up of effort while creating the business case. The foundation projects must be defined and built according to the strategic roadmap created at the whole-of-government level. These projects must be designed with the agility and scalability to incorporate future changes. The funding must provide a project's total life value costs, and allocate benefits from foundation projects to either future foundation or individual agency projects. The foundation projects must be part of a program of work with multiple projects scheduled. The funding should accommodate the higher cost of the first few foundation projects, and the calculation of benefits should be based on the overall program of work. The foundation projects are strategic, and must be aligned with business strategies and objectives for the next three to five years. They must be identified and marked in the business cases of projects done for a specific purpose. Their in-scope business capabilities and potential use within other projects must be included in the project case.

The overall budget must be allocated to two levels—foundation components and any components that are delivered using foundation components as part of the program. The whole-of-government foundation projects must be selected with the key services in mind, and where some agencies or departments will need to participate to provide different layers of information. For example, governments initiating services to provide open data could fund these as foundation projects. The responsibility of the governments extends beyond just providing the funding; it should also include creating an environment of collaboration within departments, and structure that is necessary for the success of foundation projects.

The agency-based project funding criteria should be changed to provide the services that are either specific to individual agencies, or not in foundation priorities, but essential for the specific agencies' operational requirements. The specific projects must be built according to business requirements, including agility and other architectural principles within the scope of the project. In some cases, these projects may be tactical solutions, and should be identified with a timeframe for replacing them with foundation project outcomes.

Care should also be taken that the scope of the project does not change so much that it causes costs to run over budget and delays to occur at a level that makes it ineffective. This is usually known as *scope creep* in the IT industry. Very often, objectives of a project not converted into clear requirements or requirements not fully understood by the project manager can lead to deployment delays. Sometimes, the project managers accept the changes required by the business, without considering their total downstream effect, and in the end cause the project to go over time and budget. Involving users early and starting with a proof of concept (POC) to slowly build the system are recommended. Scope creep, or scope gallop, commonly cause projects to not deliver in time and on budget, and in some cases even to be cancelled.

The funding cycle process needs to change from a reactive approach, where individual departments and divisions are required to submit their project initiative, to a proactive approach, where the whole-of-government defines a future state for the government agencies, and then decides what projects are required to reach the destination. This journey will be difficult in many jurisdictions where government departmental priorities must be balanced with whole-of-government priorities. The Citizen Services as depicted in Figure 9 must be identified, defined, and prioritised.

Just as the private sector looks at the lifecycle of the customer and has touch points in various customer life stages that cultivate customer loyalty, government must look at the citizen's life holistically. If primary education needs an overhaul to reduce unemployment, then funds should be allocated for the bigger project of overhauling education, along with creating more opportunities for employment. Just looking at unemployment rates from year to year probably will not improve the situation at the grass-root level.

Funding could be also given in parts instead of as a whole, with a governing body to keep track of the progress of the project. Funding cycles could increase to longer term and give more discretionary powers to projects. This would

Figure 8. Funding changes process

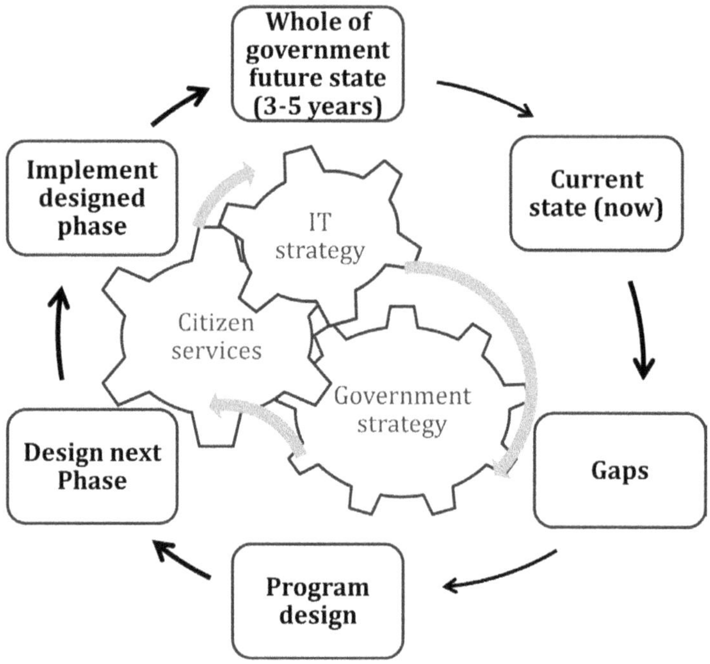

Amit Tiwary -Collaborative enterprise architecture framework©

also reduce overhead of managing the funds for each project. The allocated funding must be for the term of project, and not a definitive time or for the duration of government term.

The list of citizen services should define the government strategy to achieve these services, and plan an IT strategy to achieve them. As shown in Figure 8 the Citizen Service, IT, and government strategies must be synchronised and prioritised. These components should assist in designing the future state of whole-of-government. Expectations are that the future state will align with the political cycle for the funding process, as many governments may not commit for more than their terms in power. The maturity of this process can assist in the continuation of funding, even if the government changes and the project does not fall within its sphere of election promises.

The difficult part will be to understand the current state of organisational capabilities to provide Citizen Services. A number of assessment methods could be used, but getting a quick analysis to identify the current state is recommended. A common definition across government departments for the enterprise data models and Citizen Services must support the quick current-state assessment. The current and future steps should identify the gaps between what is currently offered as Citizen Services, and the expected services in the future state.

Transparency and accountability could be adopted by the CEAF as a foundation project. The cost of integrating these services in the system will be more than the cost of projects carried out for a specific business case, but it will reduce duplications of effort required for business case development, and other project costs from design to implementation across the organisation. Doing this as a foundation project will instill uniformity and a standard approach to the depth of access and knowledge of processes granted by the systems. Societal acceptance or attitude toward personal information and the democratic structure of the government also govern the level of transparency. Transparency promotes trust, and accountability prevents corruption by keeping processes open, encouraging more participation by the citizens, who can see how decisions are made and make more informed choices. When citizens participate in public affairs, they can help build systems that are beneficial to the society, making them happier.

Digitisation can also help reduce corruption. The Brazilian government opened its portals and published its expenditures, credit cards issued, and companies banned from contracting with the government, along with other such information that journalists are now using to expose corruption (Chui, Farrell, Jackson 2014).

In Karnataka, India, in 2001, the land records were digitised and the total amount of time to retrieve the landowner's papers fell from a few days to under an hour. This reduced bribery of local government officials to get land papers quickly World Bank brief, 2015).

WikiLeaks is another website that allows users to anonymously post whistleblowing information. Thus, transparency and the digital revolution help governments toward a better, safer, and more trustworthy government. Open data can also be used to create benchmarks that make it easy for organisations to see where they stand comparatively. Many schools in the UK pay a flat broadband fee, without comparing what they could get for their money in other arrangements. Benchmarking of broadband services has highlighted that they could reduce their costs by one third or more.

New York City has created an app known as 311, where a citizen's nonemergency issues can be reported by website, text, phone, or even Skype. Sixty percent of such issues can be resolved online, where users can also track their requests, reducing maintenance costs.

The important thing to keep in mind about transparent government is selecting information, standardisation, and when and where the data should be made available. Timely and accurate data is required to make better decisions. As the data is opened, the public can make use of it. As in the case of the Brazilian government, this can help to reduce corruption. The government can also help foster innovation using open data it has released.

The CEAF adoption will also reduce integration costs between agencies. The CEAF will reverse the downward trends in information-technology investment, providing better services with the consolidated funds, and maximising value from investments, always an imperative for governments. The CEAF adoption could provide the right resources to the project to reduce compromise on skills due to budget constraints. Through its funding model, the CEAF could allocate funds for an innovation and competency centre, or a centre of excellence that would be available to all the agencies and departments of the government. This will also encourage adoption of CEAF across multiple governments. The adoption of CEAF does demand that government be vigilant in delivering value for the investment. This will also motivate governments at all levels (i.e., local, state, or federal) to define a similar funding model and provide access to activities or projects across other jurisdictions. The information exchange will facilitate intergovernmental information sharing of project outcomes, learning, and knowledge. The Centre of Excellence concept will facilitate the adoption of new technology across governments, reducing wasted opportunities attributable to funding issues and implementation of obsolete technology. The governments could move toward Smart Services and build "tomorrow's systems today." The CEAF adoption will require providing funds for maintenance, upgrades, and project completion. This will reduce the effort required to resubmit business cases for each and every update to the application, using the current funding cycles. The benefits of the CEAF are described in Table 1.

ENTERPRISE-WIDE CITIZEN SERVICE CONCEPTS

The CEAF foundation projects should define at least the major services required for smart governments. The smart services need to define government-wide positions in the following areas:

Table 1. Using CEAF for better business investment

Government Challenges	Using CEAF
Poor initial business case	The CEAF adoption requires the enterprise-wide design of services. Such a design will assist in creating a realistic business case with a predefined outcome. The Citizen services should be designed in phases, and CEAF will provide a framework to measure the expected business outcomes. Defining the requirements on an enterprise-wide scale will enhance business-case development, and the clarity of requirements and service designs will assist in creating achievable business cases.
Unclear statements of expected outcomes	The CEAF adoption will define clear requirements and will provide a definitive intent of the project. The functionality offered by Citizen services and Information Services should be able to measure the success of the projects. The cost of providing similar services before launching CEAF on a government-wide scale, compared to the cost of these services after the adoption of CEAF, will provide an indication of the efficient use of the investment.
Lack of senior management buy-in	The CEAF adoption requires holistic government strategies defined before designing any of the services and will need to bring senior management as stakeholders to get the necessary buy-in.
Inadequate gateway reviews	The CEAF adoption will provide a mechanism to assess the investment based on government's prioritised services. The governance process as recommended in CEAF infrastructure should evaluate projects risks and provide adequate governance during planning and implementation of the initiatives.
Poor communication	The CEAF, assisted with Centre of Excellence, can build adequate skills required for better communication of intents of projects and services. The governance process should highlight any business or technology risks and communicate this to all stakeholders
Inadequate stakeholder engagement	The CEAF provides the holistic design of the services across agencies and departments that will assist in identifying and engaging right stakeholders at the right time.
Scope creep (or in many cases "scope gallop")	The CEAF should reduce any scope creep or scope gallop in projects. As services are designed holistically, the motivation to fill in known gaps by one mega project will reduce. The Centre of Excellence will also manage the scope of the projects.
Conflicts of interest	The prioritisation of service at the government level will offer enough transparency and accountability to reduce conflicts of interests. In some cases, the exposure of projects list to multiple departments will reduce opportunities for any conflicts of interests
Optimism bias when assessing prospective benefits	The program structure supported by CEAF will provide a realistic and pragmatic phasing of project designs and implementation. The program structure could also draw upon the right skills required to assess the progress of projects and provide guidance and required control to reduce "overspending" opportunities.
Group think	"Group think" will be challenged by the stakeholders representing some government divisions and departments.
Lack of appreciation of the "big picture."	CEAF adoption is based on holistic design of the government services and will provide the implementation of government strategies from top down
Decision makers being too embedded in the project so they cannot see the forest for the trees.	The program structure provides required control to reduce project-based thinking and implementation.

- **Information Management:** Information Management articulates a clear and coherent approach to the management of all government and national information, through the information management life cycle from creation to disposal. The approach is essential to enabling governments to deliver the highest quality smart services through access to accurate, timely, and relevant information.
- **Information Security:** The security of information is essential to ensuring information management consistent with both legislative obligations and achieving effective smart-government outcomes for the community.
- **Identity and Access Management (IDAM):** IDAM builds upon and extends the existing capability of ensuring that all entities requiring information from smart services have access to only the information required, in a secure, effective, and efficient manner. IDAM also enables the organisation to become more agile through the definition of business rules that take a whole-of-government view, rather than a business-unit or divisional perspective.
- **Business Intelligence and Analytics:** These provide the tools and technical platforms to analyse and interrogate all available information, regardless of location.
- **Digital Asset Management (DAM):** To deliver the value of digital assets for better policy outcomes, the effective and secure management of these digital assets from creation to disposal, using consistent practices, processes, and corporate-supported smart services must be addressed as a priority.
- **Workflow Management:** Similar to IDAM, an enterprise-level workflow management system operates across all of government's IT systems to deliver streamlined and repeatable information.

CHANGES IN PROCESSES

Disruptive technology can offer some of the checks and balances expected from transparent and accountable government services, to help reduce the number of processes for verifying the correctness and accuracy of information. The new workflow mechanism could automate the information validation and verification steps. Holistic Citizen Services could utilise multi-departmental information to validate information automatically. For example, identification of the person currently requires quite a few documents, including legal documents such as passports or driver's licenses, credit cards, or other government- or nongovernment-issued identification. These documents are then physically verified for correctness and accuracy. The CEAF can create some of these verification services using image-recognition technology, and reduce the manual steps required for verification. The personalisation of these services using information services will deliver better and quicker service with consistent processes. The CEAF service layer should reduce the elaborate, and perhaps redundant, old process replicated across multiple departments. For example, in some countries, citizen identification cards use biometrics and reduce the process steps. The same mechanism could apply in private transactions as well.

The development of the CEAF foundation projects involves various divisions, and will reduce the number of process steps at the design level, and provide optimised processes that could be implemented using foundation services. The foundation services should uniformly adopt the interpretation of the legal rules across all departments, and reduce legal, financial, resourcing, or IT/communication issues and their differing versions of adoption.

The CEAF will apply common standards to business processes, and decrease the number of failure points by encapsulation of technology by the information services. The enterprise-wide governance rules of processes and projects will reduce complexities and provide common platforms for the process changes across the government departments and agencies, encouraging a holistic approach to a program of development for the entire organisation. Table 2 depicts how CEAF will manage process challenges.

CHANGES IN WORKFORCE STRUCTURE

The development of Citizen Services should be structured as a program of work with a planned number of iterations to provide the services. The iteration cycle should be based on the functionality or integration requirements within the departments. The program structure should be funded from inception to completion of the services.

The program of work may adopt any methodology of software-development life cycle. The essential phases will be to discover the services required. The discovery phase should define required outcomes and gaps between current and expected services. The discovery activity must establish the business outcomes expected from the new service designs. The scope of the services must be defined, along with a project sponsor, business lead, and enterprise

Table 2. Managing process challenges using CEAF

Process Challenges	CEAF
Processes: Some could be outdated and have a chance to realign themselves with new expectations.	The CEAF will provide process optimisation and also realign these processes with the new technology.
Organisational structures: These could be duplicated across different departments as they work, without sharing knowledge with each other.	The processes optimisation by defining the services will reduce the organisational structure duplications.
Should be more automated decision making keeping in mind the regulatory issues Paper and manual processes To streamline processes Enforce common standards.	The workflow and automation of the processes will be required when services are defined. This should assist in streamlining processes and organisational structure to support the new processes.

Figure 9. Program structure

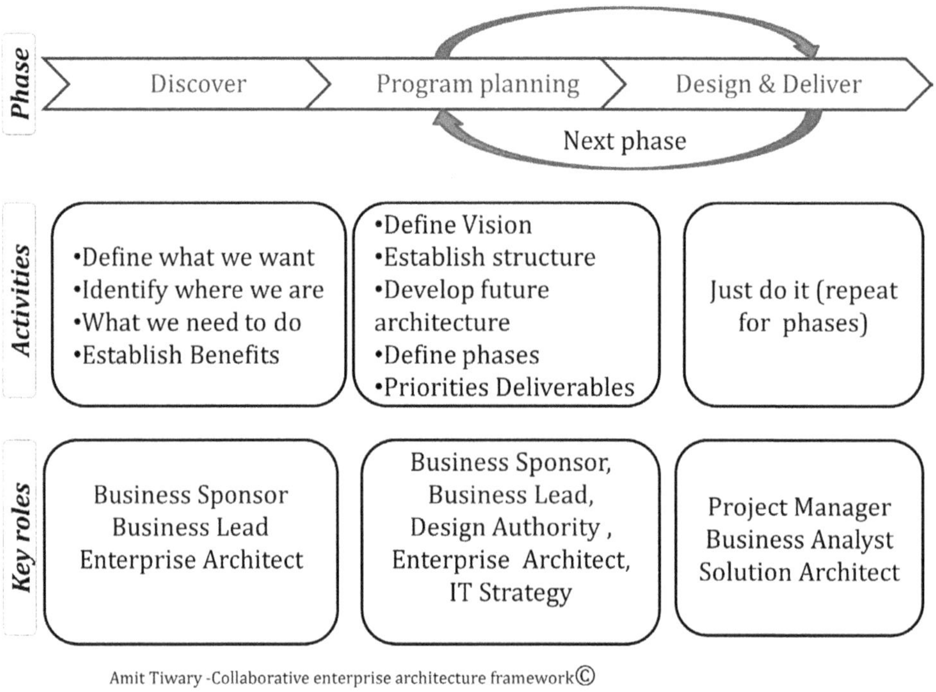

architects who can define the overall scope of the program of work. The skills in capacity planning and future planning, with up-to-date technical knowledge for implementing new technical solutions, must be hired at a government level. The concepts of a centre of excellence for each key technology could be created. In many government organisations, information technology has been partially or fully outsourced. Such cases call for realigning contracts to provide the key skills of a centre of excellence for all departmental needs.

Figure 10. Organisation structure

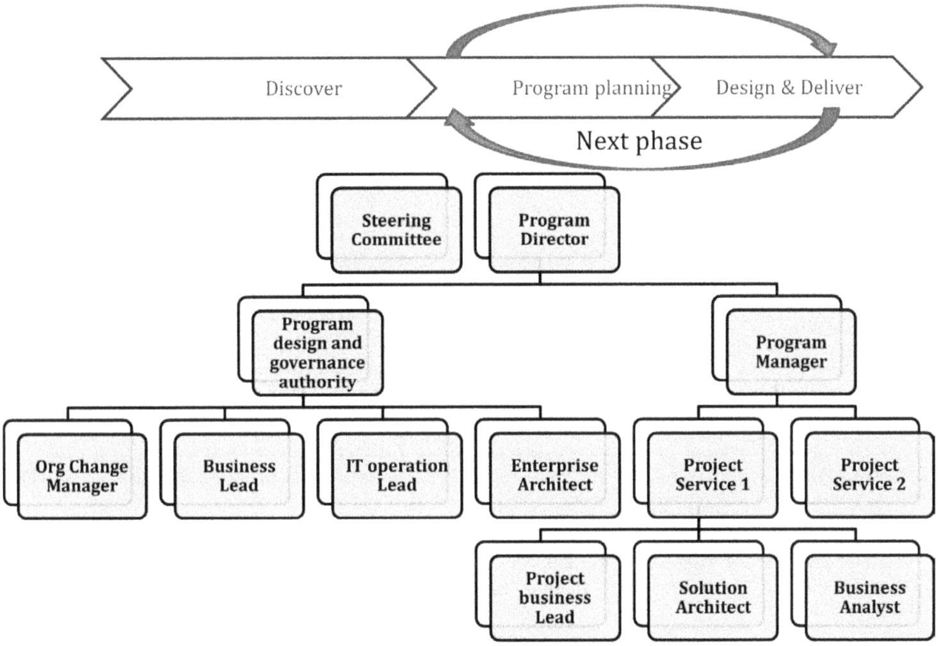

Amit Tiwary -Collaborative enterprise architecture framework©

The outsourced partners should be asked to provide the right mix of skills and capabilities needed across the government departments, for sustained growth and support of processes and projects. The program-planning phase shown in Figure 9 should establish the structure and vision, and define the structure of the program phases and deliverables. The organisational structure changes must provide skills as depicted in Figure 10.

The government sector will need to create a "special skills category," to acquire employees with the necessary skills to work in a dynamic environment, and compensate them at market rates. This will reduce dependence on expensive consultants filling in skills gaps. The CEAF provides an opportunity for the government sector to create an efficient and effective workforce that could serve all departments and divisions in common, reducing the overall cost that departments pay individually for these skill gaps. The concept of centre of excellence will make its employees feel empowered about their career, and provide an organisational structure with chances to improve their skills and opportunities for career advancement. The centre of excellence will provide a structured program of career progression, and could attract younger

Table 3. Managing team challenges using CEAF

Team Challenges	CEAF Adoption
Lack of clear roles and responsibilities result in confusion, errors, and omissions.	The CEAF framework provides clear skill requirements. The program structure could assist in defining roles and responsibilities clearly.
There are inadequate team members to complete the work that has been committed to	The holistic planning of the services will plan for provision of skills in phases where they are required. The collaborative framework will also provide funding to acquire these skills.
Projects are done "off the side of the desk" (i.e., team members do their everyday job and do the project on the side. This does not commit them to the project as a full-time resource).	The centre of excellence and holistic planning will allocate required resources to the projects.
The team does not have the necessary technical or business skills needed to complete the project successfully.	Stakeholder engagement and holistic planning of services will assist in identifying required subject matter expertise, and the funding model should provide the resources.
Employing the first available resource rather than waiting for the person with the right skills and qualifications.	The program structure and senior executive sponsorship can assist in right skills allocated to the projects.
The team is not trained in technology in use, processes it will need to know, or the business domain in which the system will run.	The training in change management engagement should provide the resources to transition to a service-based approach. The optimisation of processes will free up resources.

generations to take government jobs. The new structure will provide them opportunities for leadership development and skill advancement, and will also help build an exciting atmosphere in which younger talent can thrive. This will also mean that they can take on senior-level roles later as opportunities become available, making for smoother transitions within the organisation. Workplace conditions, praising good performance, team-building culture, and internal programs to build capabilities and skills that matter (e.g., on-the-job training, feedback on managing and risk awareness) contribute to retaining and attracting talented employees. Table 3 depicts how CEAF will assist in managing team challenges currently faced by government projects.

The new organisational structure will require defining government-wide workflow for Citizen Services. Workflow is the sequence of activities necessary to complete a task. Workflow management automates the sequencing of activities within the business process and between different departments and systems, by predetermined business rules and policies. Workflow management ensures that Citizen Services can build robust and repeatable outcomes through compliance with legislation and the optimisation of processes that enforce the appropriate allocation of tasks and approvals.

Table 4. Implementing government goals and vision using CEAF

Government Challenges	CEAF
Failure to understand why a piece of work or project is being done, before knowing what is being done. This understanding of what is wanted from the project is necessary to deliver the right results and meet the needs of the organisation.	The project will deliver well-defined services—either Citizen Services where the outcomes of the services can be measured, or internal information services for better analytics.
Failure to document and communicate the reason the project is being done, and to use it as the focal point of planning and clarity in how it will help the strategic goal.	The CEAF is driven by the government vision. The program structure will have following components: • Define vision • Establish structure • Develop future architecture • Define phases • Priorities deliverables.
Project objectives are not achieving the overall business goals and not aligned with the strategy of the organisation as a whole. The project might have a private agenda that is not following the path the company needs to take, to achieve its desired future state.	The project objectives are based on government strategy and visions. The program structure will reduce any private agenda included in the project implementation.
Project defines its vision and goals, but the definition is not used later as a guide for decision making.	The program structure and governance will keep the project vision on track, and phased approach will assist in developing required services in a planned manner. The funding of foundation projects will ensure that adequate budgets are allocated for the project's successful implementation.
Many projects on the go are not coordinated with each other on agenda and outcome. This might result in conflicting end results from the projects, not helping the government achieve its final goal.	The proposed program structure will assist in holistic planning of projects and their outcomes.
The sponsor of the project relies on the project manager to make all decisions and is not the guiding force behind the direction of the project.	The program structure and planned strategy will assist in governing the project outcomes.
Failure to give the right level of oversight support to team members. Both micromanaging and not tracking any activity in the project lead to demotivation of the team, and the project runs the possibility of not delivering.	The project and program governance with the senior executives as the stakeholders will reduce the risks of project oversight.

Workflow management allows the user/organisation to define appropriate workflows for various types of jobs or processes. At each step in the workflow, an individual or a group has responsibility for a specific task. Once the task is completed, individuals responsible for the next activity receive notification and the data they need to perform their part of the task. Once implemented, workflow management will provide an enterprise-level solution that will leverage the information-security solutions to embed repeatable task sequencing and approvals within all government processes. Table 4 defines the benefits of CEAF in managing government goals and vision.

CHANGES IN INFORMATION MANAGEMENT

Technology-based information sharing needs enthusiastic individual participation. In the absence of incentives, there might be very little participation in sharing this knowledge, rendering the platform ineffective. Structured and unstructured information must be available in the context of the knowledge and information requirements for various groups. Online portals and knowledge repositories are required to manage and make sure that information and knowledge are relevant and current. These should be reviewed and lessons applied all the time, or else they are not of much use. Information management across the government will need to change from an individual department-based approach to whole-of-government information. Information management will require a framework to define the following items:

- **Data Governance:** The CEAF adoption will need a framework to define data governance across the whole-of-government. This will require a common information management framework, implemented with a standard Business Classification Scheme for all information classification. The classification of information should apply to structured (stored in systems), unstructured, and semistructured (e-mails, reports) information. CEAF services will use this classification along with a security classification.
- **Security Governance:** This aspect of governance should be defined at all levels of information targeted for sharing. The Citizen Services should have security embedded in the information. This may require encryption of information at the source, and decrypting based only on the information requestor's security clearance.
- **Information Owners Defined for Each Information Subject Area:** An Information Owner is responsible for the management of specific information assets on behalf of the organisation. The context of the information will determine information ownership. Information owners have responsibility for:
    - Identifying impacts of legislative or organisational changes on the information requirements of the business.
    - Ensuring that appropriate security and processes, consistent with the organisational policy, are implemented for information assets.
    - Determining appropriate security classification or sensitivities of information assets and the associated access restrictions to be applied to these assets.

  - Reporting and assisting in the investigation of security breaches or issues.

The information owner is also the work-unit manager for information/records not stored in a corporate application, such as hardcopy documents or images, digital documents, or audio/visual material, whether stored on removable devices/media, personal drives, or network drives. For information/records stored in a corporate application, all information or its significant subsets have a nominated information owner responsible for management of that information on behalf of the organisation. The information owner's approval must be sought whenever there is a request to access, modify, or enhance information held in an application. Application information owners must represent an appropriate appointment for that level of responsibility, and occupy a position of sufficient authority to make decisions on behalf of the organisation to fulfil this obligation. The information owner must be a senior executive accountable for ensuring that matters relating to their allocated information entities meet the organisation's needs and requirements. This includes providing advice and direction to information, application, policy, and process owners, as required.

- **Information Custodians:** Individuals with this responsibility provide governance, maintenance of information sources, and input to policy, process, and application. They advise on use of the information, including legislative changes, and initiate reviews of issues relating to their subject areas, in consultation with various departments. Their role also includes monitoring and evaluating the information subject areas to ensure that any changes relating to those are effective, address related risks, and meet organisational needs and requirements.
- **Policy Owner:** Policy Owners are department or divisional heads responsible for undertaking or coordinating day-to-day business relating to their allocated policy subjects. This includes:
  - Providing input into policy advice on the subject, including legislative change, or any other changes required for the policies, mapped to any business-capability changes.
  - Initiating reviews of policy issues relating to their subject, in consultation with Strategy and Policy. Reviews may be in response to general monitoring of the subject, risk assessments, internal or external reviews, or continuous improvement activities.

- ◦ Assessing policy proposals initiated by other employees or work units, and preparing policy-development plans for the conduct of policy reviews, whether initiated by themselves or other organisational units, or directed by the Accountable Officer. This is done in collaboration with Strategy and Policy.
- ◦ Overseeing the conduct of policy reviews and providing advice or direction on the recommendation of reviews. Ensuring that policy change is properly implemented includes identifying implementation requirements and associated costs and coordinating their delivery.
- ◦ Monitoring and or evaluating the subject to make sure that any related policies are effective, address associated risks, and meet organisational needs and requirements.

- **Service Owner:** The individual in this role is accountable for managing the services outcome and process, and its objectives as implemented by Information Services; and ensuring that it is fit for its purpose according to agreed-upon and documented standards, and meets the aim of the process definition.
- **System Owner:** The System Owner for corporate applications and IT infrastructure is ultimately responsible for the secure management and support of critical information on behalf of the organisation. Hence, system owners of applications or IT infrastructure must be an appropriate appointment for that level of responsibility, and in a position of sufficient authority to make decisions on behalf of the organisation.

The CEAF Information Management Framework (IMF) will enable understanding of what information is needed by government stakeholders; the information owner; where that information is stored; in what format it needs to be stored; its security classification; and who can access it.

The CEAF information framework must also guide defining processes to improve data quality and easy integration between systems. The service framework could assist in data quality improvement initially at the service layer, and then flow back the updated quality of data to source systems. For example, if the service layer is required to translate information about the address and add geospatial coordinates, these coordinates should also be updated in source systems. This mechanism will avoid a full update of the legacy systems data, but over time could achieve the quality of data that is required by services. The service layer should define system processes to tighten security and privacy of data in a hybrid data environment, align data to business needs, and provide timeliness of information in contextual information availability. The CEAF framework should reduce the business cost of storing and retrieving information over time, and provide an enterprise view of information and its effects on enterprise information governance. Enterprise governance of systems will assist in decommissioning of independent systems, and reduce islands of information. The differentiation between transactional information and analytical information will diminish, and Information Services should synchronize information across systems and departments. The CEAF adoption and definition of roles and responsibilities will assist in managing stakeholder issues with project outcomes. Table 5 defines managing stakeholder's engagement issues with CEAF.

Table 5. Managing stakeholder engagement issues with CEAF

Government Challenges	CEAF
Failure to determine the right stakeholders and engage them subsequently (classic mistake award winner)	The holistic planning of the services and adoption of CEAF reduces the risk of not engaging right stakeholders. The program approach and designing of the services up front will require all the stakeholders to be engaged with right representation.
Failing to look at the project through the eyes of stakeholders and keep their benefit in the forefront of the decisions. This might result in stakeholders being negatively impacted by the decisions made.	The service's design, based on the business outcomes, will provide stakeholders what they need, rather than what an IT project guessed were their requirements. The program structure and engagement of the key stakeholders will reduce the risks of designing and implementing the project without adequate consultation with business for their requirements.
Imposing a solution or decision on stakeholders and failing to get their buy-in.	The key stakeholder is engaged in the program of work from the inception of the projects. The centre of excellence will also provide opportunities to the stakeholders participating in key decision making processes.
Failing to listen to all stakeholders and letting the most vocal ones take over the decision making.	The holistically designed services will reduce the dominance of one vocal group.
Failure to ensure that training the stakeholders to use the new product is included as in-scope of the project. The new ways of working introduced by the project must be understood by the stakeholders for the project changes to be utilised and successful.	The program structure will provide adequate resources required for the change management activities. Participation of the key stakeholders and appropriate governance will also provide an opportunity to manage the IT changes and organisational changes.
Failure to ensure sufficient and effective communications between the team members involved in the project (classic mistake award winner).	The program structure and inclusion of change managers as part of program will assist in communication of changes in timely manner.

CHANGES IN KNOWLEDGE MANAGEMENT

Knowledge management and analytics refer to a set of tools and techniques that transform large volumes of data into meaningful information that can help and direct strategic and tactical decision making. Knowledge management and analytics processes encompass all aspects of data accessibility, integration, management, analysis, and deployment, to allow decision makers at all levels to receive and act upon relevant integrated information in real time. It is a search for the "one single version of the truth" that can be elusive in operational activities that currently have multiple individual groups of data and information management systems. Knowledge management will require a sea of change in all participating departments and agencies. Information services, although designed for the use of the Citizen, must also serve the knowledge-management needs of each department. The needs and characteristics of these two user categories are based on a three-pillars approach, depicted in Figure 11.

Figure 11. Pillars of knowledge management

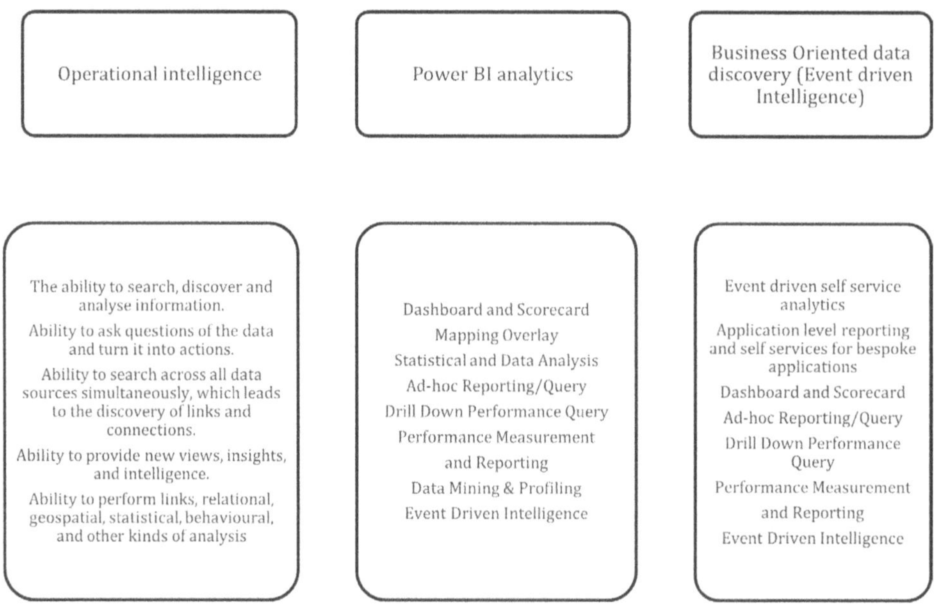

Amit Tiwary -Collaborative enterprise architecture framework©

- **Pillar One:** Operational Intelligence (OI). OI is dynamic and real time business analytics that delivers insight into operations of the business. This analytics gives live visibility into the operations of the enterprise, still needs a foundation level power BI and self-service to assist and build static reports and patterns that these systems can use. The information services should be designed to meet the operational needs of the participating departments. In many cases, the operational context of the information may change, but the agile design of services could be used for all operational needs of the departments and agencies. For example, if a service is defined to associate cases with persons and actions, it could be used in law enforcement, as well as for health-related operational intelligence. The source of data may change to law-enforcement data if the requestor is from the Police, or to health data if the requestor is from the health department.
- **Pillar Two:** Power BI and analytics. Each organisation and the whole-of-government need heavy-duty analysis capability. Under this scenario, Power Users would continue to provide the following specialised services:
  - Statistical Reporting to various departmental, other government agencies;
  - Ad Hoc Reporting (Ministerial, Regional, Divisional, Media);
  - Performance Measurement;
  - Key Performance Indicators (KPI) Analysis;
  - Forecasting;
  - Profiling;
  - Investigations;
  - Data extracts to interstate and national bodies (Corporate Statistics Agency); and
  - Publications Production/Annual Report (Performance Measures),
- **Pillar Three:** Business-oriented data discovery (event-driven intelligence). Medium-size reporting and self-services need to have another product with reporting capability that reduces the bespoke system reporting costs, and also utilises enterprise-wide reporting capabilities. With analysis and reporting undertaken at the Business Unit, Divisional, Regional, and Station levels, business users can create their own real-time or ad hoc analysis, so that they can perform "what-if" analyses and build charts, reports, graphs, and dashboards to meet the departmental or local need. Knowledge management needs to establish an enterprise-wide architecture to accommodate self-

service analytics that satisfy data governance, security, and integrity requirements that ensure best practice is disseminated across the organisation, and promote efficiency.

TECHNOLOGY UPGRADE USING CEAF

The CEAF adoption by government departments will initially encapsulate many legacy systems, and provide a roadmap to modernize applications with a planned approach. CEAF adoption should simplify some of the processes for approvals and funding, assisting government to modernize and build agile systems to meet new challenges faced by governments across the globe. CEAF should provide a platform to realign with new technology capabilities, and the CEAF framework could develop services once and deploy them across departments and agencies, reducing development and implementation cycles. CEAF funding and service costs can assist in utilising taxpayer money efficiently.

CEAF could adopt a "Bi-model" approach to developing systems with agile and waterfall methods. To facilitate the adoption of CEAF, the design and definition of the enterprise architecture should assist in defining common platforms for Information and Citizen Services, covering areas of Business Intelligence and Analytics; Geospatial Infrastructure, databases, integration, and data repository; Identity and Access Management; Enterprise Storage; and Network Infrastructure.

At the presentation layer, design and development of an employee, citizen, and interagency portal should provide the entry point and user interface to access each Information and Citizen Services gate. Each Information and Citizen Service Portal should provide individual department-employee service, where an employee can access all information and services based on roles and responsibilities. That access should be systems agnostic; a Citizen portal, where citizens can exchange information with government departments using predefined processes and services; within an Interagency layer that will exchange information based on predefined exchange Memorandums Of Understanding (MOUs) and services. A memorandum of understanding (MOU or MoU):is a formal agreement between two or more parties. This will provide secure and real-time information to the interagencies, reducing the need for storing information at each agency level.

The CEAF will present information contextually at the information-management layer. The enterprise data model, which describes information requirements for people, objects, locations, and events, developed on a concurrent basis by participating agencies. This must be and aligned to the enterprise data model. The enterprise data model is essential, as it allows the presentation layer to access accurately and promptly the information required for the services. At the services layer, the investment will enable the definition and design of the foundation services, which include at the base level:

- Identity and access service (providing role-based, streamlined access to applications and network-stored information);
- Geospatial Service (Web-mapping service, geocoding, reverse geocoding, address validation);
- Digital Asset Management (basic service operations to provide storage and retrieval).

Finally, at the Infrastructure layer, the following will be addressed:

- Design and establish Business Intelligence infrastructure;
- Establish geospatial infrastructure and databases, and integrate with applications;
- Establish Identity and Access Management infrastructure;
- Design and implement storage infrastructure; and
- Redesign and optimise Enterprise Network.

Regarding interdependencies, the presentation, information management, services, and infrastructure cannot be decoupled, as each layer is essential to delivering the proposed outcomes. Table 6 describes how CEAF will meet these challenges.

CEAF-BASED GOVERNANCE

Governance is the overall management approach that monitors and controls projects in organisations, so as to keep sight of the big picture and deliver value. Governance must understand both the strategy and the limitations of the organisation to make sensible, cost-effective, and appropriate decisions. Governance is usually top down. The priorities of the business, based on its capabilities, can be approved and accepted by the organisation when it comes from the decision makers and owners of the organisation. Effective governance is built on a body that comprises both business and technical decision makers

Table 6. Managing architecture and design challenges using CEAF

Architecture and Design Challenges	CEAF
Allowing a pet idea to become the chosen solution without considering if other solutions might meet the project's overall goal in a better way.	The CEAF adoption requires governance based on the government vision and enterprise strategy. This will reduce the instances of pet solutions being implemented. The governance process and program structure will reduce the possibility of solution implementation at an independent, unintegrated level.
Teams develop individual parts of the project without looking at the overall needs and architecture of the project. The result, in this case, might not be able to integrate together, rendering the project inefficient and expensive to operate.	The CEAF provides visibility of enterprise-wide priorities and also designs the services collaboratively. This will reduce the risk of individual components implemented without thought having been given to how they will be integrated into the bigger picture.
Failure to take into account all requirements, especially performance requirements, results in an end product that is operationally unusable.	The CEAF layers will assist in defining the service level expected, and include functional and nonfunctional requirements across the program.
Bad architecture which is difficult to maintain, and hard to debug.	The enterprise-level design will assist in providing optimal solutions to all stakeholders.
Being lured into using new technology even if it is not required.	The prioritisation of the project based on government strategy and vision will reduce the risk of implementing unnecessary solutions.
The developer is creating extra features that are not required, making the system unnecessarily complex and knowledge expensive.	Scope and phasing will assist in defining the requirements up front. Governance should assess each requirement against the outcomes expected, and thus manage the gold plating.
Failure to use the right tools for the right jobs, and using the one that is known by the team. This known tool might not be the panacea, the right tool for all project needs	The CEAF allows for multiple solutions and will reduce one-size-fits-all solutions.
The team does not have the right training for a new tool, and the task-completion progress is not reported accurately. When the developer believes the task is 90% complete, he/she might not have enough knowledge to know that the rest of the tasks will take as long as the initial 90%	The program phased approach and centre of excellence structure should assist in acquiring necessary skills with all new technology implementation.

of the organisation. It is a two-way learning process between legislatives and agencies executives. A good governing body can help steer projects in the right direction, especially when conflicts arise. At the same time, governance is about continuously improving, tracking, and monitoring its model as well, so that it delivers better results each time. Government projects have many unique hurdles, and their governance has its challenges. Governance also advances confidence in the business when it is done with responsibility and direction. Governance should make clear who is responsible and for what, as well as ensuring that responsible parties have the expertise to make the decision. A person with the requisite expertise would be:

- The highest authority and final arbiter on matters concerning BI and Analytics within the government IT organisation;
- Accountable for driving future BI strategy and defining data ownership, including making decisions on data sources to be integrated and fed into the data warehouse.

Data experts will bring specialist knowledge and expertise around data from their specific business area. They are data stewards responsible for the quality, security, and availability of data, and for ensuring compliance with relevant policies, principles, standards, and procedures. They carry out the duties of managing and protecting the data for their respective data owners.

BI tools will bring knowledge and expertise in BI-related tool sets that include ETL tools, data-profiling and data-quality tools, OLAP (Online Analytic Processing, often is used in data mining. It is analysis done on data stored in the enterprise) and information delivery tools, and data-mining tools. Once the BI governance structure has been established, the following BI-related policies, principles, and standards will be developed, promulgated, and applied:

- BI data-management policies (covering the entire data life cycle of data extraction, storage, quality, availability, retention, backup, archiving, recovery, and purging);
- BI data-security policies;
- BI architectural principles;
- BI data-quality standards; and
- BI naming conventions.

The government should start by restructuring how it manages public money. It could refine the budgeting, investment, and revenue process, so it can be more transparent about where departments can reduce their expenditures, and how they can change the criteria for collection of income. It can also optimise its capital allocation, management, and assurance processes.

The government should collaborate on analytical capabilities between departments to understand economic efficiency at a unit-cost level. The government sometimes approves huge, complex, multiyear projects with a single business case. As a result, major projects tend to layer in high-level risk adjustments, distorting capital-allocation decisions. In contrast, some of the most effective private companies encourage investment discipline by breaking down large projects into chunks and stages.

Finally, while major capital investments go through both departmental reviews and the Treasury's gate-based review process, managing the productivity of capital expenditure often lacks attention. The new unified system enables the government to improve its management of spending cuts by improving efficiency. By centralising IT operations, delivering the e-government services and shared services will enable economies of scale, increase efficiency, and enhance service levels to increase customer satisfaction. Apart from this, the consolidation of services and applications highlights IT infrastructure and need for new skills, providing more attractive careers and cross-government work that improves skills. Succeeding in shared services will require an understanding of not only where the value lies, but also how to capture it through careful centralisation of relevant services at the right level of aggregation. Shared services bring about greater collaboration and productivity enhancements. The unified system improves fraud management and increases government savings. In these times of increasing pressure for budgetary savings, this kind of integration of government at national, regional, and local levels is both required and desirable.

REFERENCES

Chui, M., Farrell, D., & Jackson, K. (2014, April). *How government can promote open data and help unleash over $3 trillion in economic value.* Digital McKinsey.

NIEM. (2014). Retrieved from https://www.niem.gov/

Park, J., & Hwang, J. (2003). Role-based Access Control for Collaborative Enterprise in Peer-to-Peer Computing Environments. *Proceedings of the Eighth ACM Symposium on Access Control Models and Technologies.*

World Bank Brief. (2015, Oct 26). *Digitizing Land Records in Karnataka India.* Retrieved from http://www.worldbank.org/en/topic/governance/brief/digitising-land-records-in-karnataka-india

Chapter 4
CEAF Implementation Roadmap

ABSTRACT

Working collaboratively and providing Citizen Services on a whole-of-government model require intensive resources, planning a methodology, and support by senior executives. This, in turn, requires extensive electronic and mobile collaboration. The rapidity of global communications has certainly influenced the world's view of leadership toward seeing collaboration as an effective and efficient way to provide necessary services to citizens. This is also an intelligent way of looking at governments. Open-data initiatives will require a higher level of cooperation within and among government departments. The extent of changes and avoidance of various pitfalls for this implementation need to be thought through within governments and with external organisations.

INTRODUCTION

The CEAF roadmap requires a planned approach for successful implementation. The key challenges, such as funding cycle, process, and technology implementation issues, must be analysed in the context of the governments and the political cycles. In many circumstances, local governments are keen to invest in initiatives closer to elections. The CEAF roadmap must disengage from funding cycle variations. It should be considered the foundation of the local government services, and must be funded for a defined period of time.

DOI: 10.4018/978-1-5225-2407-6.ch004

Defining the roadmap will require a catalogue of the services expected from local governments in the short, medium, and long term. A current assessment of "where we are" should follow, and this assessment should highlight the gaps between the current state and the "to-be" state. The roadmap must define the prioritisation of the initiatives that allocated budgets could fund. CEAF should also provide opportunities to save on the costs of serving its citizens. Savings from the adoption of the CEAF should flow back to the planned initiative, and at some stage it should become self-funding from the savings.

ROADMAP PLANNING

Get Key Stakeholders Involved or in Charge

The CEAF adoption roadmap must indicate the business value and the strategic or tactical business benefits the government departments and agencies are planning to achieve. The simple fact is that the CEAF plan requires a "business metric," not an IT metric, for delivery of the application. The business must define the main benefits it expects from the CEAF. Key areas for improvement are information management framework processes; the technology supporting them; and the culture of the organisation. The business must evaluate the key services—integration processes—and optimise them before initiating any IT projects. The existing organisational culture within various departments must be analysed and factored into the roadmap.

Allow Ample Time for Evaluation and Planning

The CEAF will require a high-level analysis, and then a detailed analysis of current business processes, cultures, and IT-systems topology. Ample time must be allocated to building a robust roadmap. The projects should be recommended based on the roadmap, and will require a clear vision for the next three to five years, which must be included in the program of work of multiple years. This will require a change in process from the current annual program of work for two to three years, to a program of work for the foundation projects.

Have a Big Vision, but Take Small Steps

The CEAF needs the vision and its components defined before starting any technology projects. The "big picture" must include the "to-be" processes, organisation, and any cultural refinement required. Once the big picture is defined, a well-planned phased approach is required to optimise the gain from technology enhancement, and refining of processes and organisational structure.

Consider Potential Performance Problems

Due to organic growth, the information distribution and complexity of each system might require many conversions of information before the new system can use it directly. This may create performance problems in accessing the data (i.e., transactional as compared to analytical data). The roadmap should consider any possible performance problems and design services, and processes to address them.

Institute Data Governance Policies and Processes

Data security, including permission, security, and access control of departmental data and standardisation of systems, will require establishing government-wide security policies (e.g., who can access what information, and how). This should begin with an audit of all user (employee, citizen, interagency) permissions, security of systems, and business rules for accessing customer data. Developing a comprehensive, correct, and consistent standard for all services should be a top priority. This will require standardisation of the business rules and data formats across services. Data quality improvement must be included as "business as usual" tasks to keep the data "clean" and maintain ongoing quality. This requires defining an end-to-end data-quality process and implementation, and should be an integral part of the single-customer view strategy.

Context-sensitive information must be clearly defined to assist in developing entities required for citizen and information services. Data entities must be defined as mandatory elements that should be available (e.g., name, address, telephone), others that may be considered necessary (e.g., email address, credit worthiness, contract status), and optional data that could be useful (e.g., last contact date, customer score, preferences).

DEVELOPING A ROADMAP

Once government strategies and priorities have been decided, the overall roadmap should be planned and structured. Technological change is exponential nowadays, and with the increasing importance of standardised data, government departments and agencies almost inevitably have several current initiatives at different stages of implementation that involve Citizen Information. This is both an opportunity and a risk. The roadmap should highlight benefits of aligning and enabling multiple initiatives across government departments. This will require the senior executives of the departments owning these initiatives to participate in CEAF adoption. The senior executives have to communicate the benefits to their project teams and, in some cases, delay or stop the project to ensure alignment with the whole-of-government strategic directions. The requested services may be delivered simply by coordinating the data streams in existing projects. If interdependencies are not given due consideration early enough, any new Citizen Services initiative will become another singular project, struggling to gain attention and perhaps missing an opportunity to harmonise existing initiatives.

Building a Program Plan

Once a roadmap is laid out, a program plan of projects can be built for services to be delivered in phases. This should be built keeping in mind all the classic program-management disciplines—for example, setting objectives, defining activities, measure/trial/measure, and plan/do/review approaches using the RACI method for accountability. It is important that process and people elements be considered along with information and technology. The project team must work through each of the steps from people, process, data, and technology perspectives to understand the root causes for collaboration among departments being invisible today. The work should define the current challenges the government's departments face, and align with the CEAF.

Continuous Improvement

The most significant reason for implementing a CEAF is the strategic imperative for reducing duplication in IT investment and providing better collaboration between departments and agencies. Upon completion of an initial project, limitless opportunities arise to improve and update processes, and add more information to the services.

BUILDING ROADMAPS

The roadmap based on Information and Citizen Services should be seen as the foundation of the initiative to implement CEAF across government departments. The building of foundation services will require investment and resources allocated diligently, to be agile and adaptable to changing service needs and technological advances. The CEAF adoption must be planned for services that are prioritised by the government. If the government priorities include adoption of "Open data" and "My data," these services could become initial candidates for the CEAF adoption. The services must also be planned in phases, each of which should include the functionality of adding information from a limited number of departments or agencies. For example, in the initial phases, "My data" services may only include data for education and health, and in subsequent phases add data from law enforcement and various registration bodies. This approach provides opportunities for other agencies to build macroservices for internal consumption that the CEAF services layer can use later. In building these macroservices, the current state should just define the current status of required services. The "to-be" state must be defined based on strategic goals. The roadmaps will define the steps required to achieve the desired goals. The adoption of CEAF should be considered continuous improvement, and a standard process framework should be defined for the assessment.

1. A current-state assessment requires the creation of templates for the collection of data, assessment criteria, and information assessment. These templates must be business-focused and understood by the operational team members. The templates may be refined constantly, and the process of defining them should be quick and simple.
2. The assessment of the individual layers of the CEAF should be done with service and infrastructure layers first, to ensure that the participating department or agency has foundation layers defined for CEAF adoption. The individual departmental roadmap should invest resources in defining this framework. The framework should be agile, to accommodate new services.
3. Organisational acceptance of the services gaps is required. There must be an enterprise-wide approach to developing these services, to meet individual and whole-of-government goals and strategies.

4. The desired or "to-be" state must articulate the services required to achieve the business outcomes. This must be documented and aligned with strategies. Desired outcomes must govern the activities required to deliver the to-be capabilities.
5. A plan to transition from the "current system" approach to the "desired service" approach for delivering service to the customer is required, to streamline activities and reap enterprise-wide benefits of business outcomes.
6. Governing the activities identified for building the services must use enterprise-wide governance.

The roadmap will require decision makers to consider a plan to achieve government's promised services, while departments reflect on the strategic approach to keeping these promises. The recommended program approach to adopt CEAF should define processes, policies, and templates for the following items:

- Senior executives from the departments and agencies require definition of government information and a Citizen Services catalogue. The executives, along with government representatives, must agree on government directions for the next two to three years. The foundation funding required for keeping government promises should be budgeted and allocated. The program structure must be defined and adequate resources allocated, with representation from the participating departments. The program structure should avoid limiting representation to one department or agency. The governance process for the program must be defined. The process must be transparent and accountable, with adequate resources and the right skills allocated.
- Formal templates should define Project Initiatives, with considerations for assessment and prerequisites of the initiative. This will require changes in funding cycle, which, in turn, may create an environment where initiative assessment takes most of the resources, and implementation suffers. On the other hand, some organisational processes may be restrictive, and ideas might have to go through so many assessment steps that it discourages employees from socialising any idea. In some cases, business departments could implement IT-related ideas, creating a shadow IT presence. The organisation

must define a process to encourage responsible idea generation and assessment process to avoid such situations.

- A well-defined measurement criterion for assessing any idea is required, where ideas are assessed by the benefit they provide to the whole organisation. This criterion should not be used as a camouflage for delaying tasks if demand for initiative assessment is delaying and hampering the implementation of ideas.
- The organisational prioritisation of the idea should be well defined and agreed upon across the organisation. The prioritisation criteria must be socialised within the organisation for the idea creators. The criteria may change based on organisational vision, business prioritisation, and business capabilities required to achieve the vision.

DEFINE CEAF ADOPTION VISION

The vision of the CEAF adoption must be based on two common factors. The first should be identifying the services governments must provide to constituents now. The second factor should be based on an assessment of structural change these services will require over time, due to new demands related to technological advancements. Environmental changes require constant updates of CEAF strategies. The government should have a dashboard for reporting vision realisation. This should occur not only at the senior executive level, but also embedded in organisational performance measurements.

The key challenges in the measurement of the CEAF values are quantifying intangible benefits, isolating and accruing the benefits attributable to IT investments, establishing a baseline for value measurement, and estimating value generated from foundational and support spending. Further challenges lie in communicating value using an effective vocabulary of business terms, and finding appropriate forums to discuss CEAF value with the right stakeholders. The key metrics are decreased costs, increased productivity, increased revenue, increased ROI, IT operation returns, foundational investment, portfolio prioritisation, and business value creation. Measurement and communication are separate activities, both with unique challenges, but of equal importance. Types of measurement methodologies vary with the value-measurement challenges faced.

START WITH THE END IN MIND

The investment roadmap should be initiated to achieve the strategic goals and vision that governments define. The roadmap should prioritise adoption of various layers of the CEAF within departmental information processing and common use. The current-state assessment goals are used to understand areas of concern and proactively invest in mitigating organisational and operations risks. The organisation should have these initiatives as a detailed program of work. The development of Citizen Services should be structured as a program of work with a planned number of iterations to provide the services. The iteration cycle could be based on the functionality or integration requirements within the departments. The program structure should be funded from inception to completion of the services.

A sample program structure should be created for developing business capabilities-based roadmaps. The investment roadmap should be divided into phases, such as discovery or planning what needs to be done, describing the current state of business capabilities, and identifying expected business outcomes. The organisation should invest in creating standard templates that are reusable and acceptable across the organisation. These templates should define criteria for initiating business capability-building activities, funding available, and key outcomes expected. The organisational structure should also provide stability to the program, assigning key roles and responsibilities based on the business outcomes. Senior executives must support the structure of the program, and the scope of the program should be clear.

Any standard method will suffice to develop the program of work, but discovering the need for services is indispensable. The discovery phase should define required outcomes and gaps between current and expected services. The discovery activity must establish the business outcomes expected from the new service designs. The scope of the services must be defined, and a project sponsor, business lead, and enterprise architects who can define the overall scope of the program of work identified. The skills in capacity planning and future planning with up-to-date technical knowledge for implementing new technical solutions must be hired at a government level. The concepts of centre of excellence for each of the key technologies could be created. Many government organisations have partially or fully outsourced IT, and they must realign these outsourced contracts to provide the key skills within the centre of excellence for all departmental needs. Outsourcing partners should be asked to provide the right mix of skills and capabilities that will be needed across the government departments, for sustained growth and support of processes and projects.

To acquire necessary skills to work in a dynamic environment, the government will need to create a special-skills category. CEAF provides an opportunity for the public sector to create an efficient and effective workforce common to all departments and divisions. This will reduce overall cost of departments currently paying individually to fill these skill gaps.

ANALYSE SERVICES CATALOGUE

A services catalogue must be created for all departments and agencies within governments. This should cover the most prominent services requested by citizens, interagency entities, and employees. The analysis of the service catalogue will identify common services from each department, and should be used to prioritise foundation and individual departmental services. The analysis phase should be pragmatic, and include assessment sufficient to satisfy the CEAF adoption roadmap requirements. Various dimensions may require different focus, based on the required outcome. The assessment should be time bound to avoid "analysis paralysis." The service-selection decision should enable a culture of sharing knowledge within IT. The services development should facilitate sharing of knowledge among employees within different departments.

DO A QUICK ANALYSIS OF THE ORGANISATION'S CURRENT STATE

Roadmap building will require knowing where the organisation is in its current state of maturity toward adopting the CEAF. As suggested, starting with the end in mind, the analysis of the current state will identify the gaps between current and future states. It will also define the path of building roadmap initiatives to achieve the end state. The current-state assessment should avoid documenting every current process. The assessment team should take a quick inventory of current assets, such as technology in use and people skills, and also check the mapping of capabilities with services. This approach should be defined as part of the initial assessment. The stakeholder's assessment should pick the right roles and tools for this exercise. The various options for this evaluation of current-state capability, such as surveys, desktop appraisal, or interviews, should be considered based on the availability of resources. The organisational culture must be understood by the team (internal or external consultants) so as to ask the right questions to collect the right data from the stakeholders in the assessment. The openness of the culture and acceptance of individual opinions will decide how the questions should be framed to get the facts.

MANAGE OVERALL STAKEHOLDER ENGAGEMENT IN CURRENT-STATE EVALUATION

The assessment of the current state and service maturities will require managing input from a large number of stakeholders. This will include the key business drivers of vision and outcomes, collected from senior executives to operational-level input. The level of input required will depend on how many services are assessed and the scope of the assessment. The foundation program must invest in defining standard templates for data gathering, analysis and dynamic roadmaps, assessment criteria, and measurement criteria. The foundation program must develop a stakeholder-engagement plan, from data gathering to the socialisation of its results. The assessment criteria and data-collection process must be defined and should be transparent. The assessment method will require information collection to be accurate to the ground realities, and data should not be adjusted according to preferences of senior executives or other stakeholders. That would cause feelings of distrust toward future evaluations, and may result in the prioritisation of the wrong service or fail to achieve the goals of the business outcomes expected from the investment.

DEFINING SCOPE OF TRANSFORMATION

Pragmatically achievable business outcomes must define the transformation scope. The program management must assess and determine the affordability of the program by assessing overall budget, now and for the next few years. The organisation must separately assess requirements for everyday operational activities and strategic ventures. The resources required for developing the roadmap and "keeping lights on," or the operation running, must be allocated appropriately.

COMMON INFORMATION MANAGEMENT

The common information management will have standardised information definitions and services to extract, reformat, and present information. The assumptions are that the design will avoid expensive data movements from independent systems to another data warehouse. The key benefits are:

- Standardising reporting across divisions will assist in the consolidation of information for summarisation and reporting.
- Common information on organisational information entities will be available.
- Centralised information enables operational optimisation.
- Common information management improves information accuracy and quality.
- The number of interfaces required between systems to provide the same level of reporting functionality to divisions is reduced.
- Costs of system licenses infrastructure, system support, training, and system upgrades are reduced
- The proliferation of systems is less likely.
- Systems are utilised for their capabilities.

Common information management will provide the framework for the following:

- **Aggregation (Bringing Information Together):** Information from a variety of real-time and diverse back-end data sources, automation systems, operational databases, information systems, relational database systems, and manually entered data is combined. The data is accessible to various roles based on the context. The designs and method for implementing these layers are discussed later in the book.
- **Contextualisation:** Functional/operational relationships between data elements from disparate sources are created and maintained. It may be useful, for example, to maintain relationships (context) between particular named processes.
- **Analysis:** Data is transformed into real-time performance intelligence through the application of business rules (i.e., calculated KPIs and their range, using raw performance measures and cost-based information from ERP and other business-level systems).

- **Propagation:** Relevant operational performance information is automatically transferred to the appropriate business-level systems (e.g., enterprise asset management, ERP, supply chain management, or product lifecycle management).
- **Visualisation:** Graphical representations are provided of KPIs that support the context or role-based navigation of information, based on persistent interrelationships. This will enable drill-down from multioperational to individual facilities and systems.

STANDARDISATION OF REPORTING

Each division and application may have developed its infrastructure, format, and systems for divisional and department-level reporting. This results in multiple reporting formats and duplication of effort. A substantial percentage of time is spent in collection and formatting of the reports. In addition to divisional or departmental effort, corporate sections have to employ additional resources to align these reports with the corporate format. This necessitates standardised reporting across the whole-of-government departments. It is important to utilise information services that are developed as part of CEAF adoption, to achieve the required standardisation.

KNOWLEDGE AND INTELLIGENCE MANAGEMENT ROADMAP

Business Intelligence (BI) provides insights into organisational capabilities, and bridges the gap between the vision of the organisation and its execution strategies. BI, however, needs to be extended beyond the organisation and into the collaborative space Goel, Tiwary, Schmidt 2010). Such CI is where multiple organisations/departments within an organisation share their business intelligence for win-win outcomes, without compromising their legislative roles and responsibilities. Such collective BI was evident during the recent global financial crisis, when many governments coordinated response across many cross-sections of various industries. This is achieved by correlating seemingly unrelated pieces of information that may reside unattached to other systems. For example, a hospital may have information on a group of patients who have been suffering from a certain type of cancer. An apparently unrelated piece of information hidden away elsewhere may come from their residential postcode (i.e., area of living). Correlating these two types of information may provide an insight into the nature of that geographical area and its potential relationship to the cause of cancer. From a technology perspective, collaborations require the ability to ask the right questions of business; and the business to be able to concur or deny, sensibly, the emerging value.

Collaborations require a move away from only assessing internal data on the organisation's performance, to strategising to incorporate external data (big data, including social and mobile media in various formats) relevant to organisational operations. The breathtaking rapidity of growth in communications, storage, and analytics leads to the strategic viewpoint that collaboration is a much better way of providing holistic government services.

Knowledge that correlates information groups provides insights to users, who can then use that knowledge in an appropriate way. Intelligence further abstracts the knowledge and, at the same time, provides actionable insights regarding predictive behavior. Insurance organisations can correlate hospital admissions with income levels, and thereby bring about a potential reduction in insurance costs through appropriate distributions of the client base. These scenarios depict the creative and dynamic use of data, information, and knowledge, taken from varied sources. Such use of BI & CI requires a robust CEAF adoption. Contemporary business architecture and business Intelligence and business architecture (BA/BI) needs to evolve to handle the following:

- Creation of a common language and taxonomy of architectures and solutions within the organisation;
- Creation of an enterprise information management framework;
- Ongoing alignment of data to needs of the business;
- Separation of data categories (structured and unstructured; transactional and analytical);
- Having well-organised and well-documented processes for enhancement of data quality;
- Improved integration between systems;
- Design of security and privacy of data, especially when the information is coming from disparate sources and data could be open or closed;
- Quality and timeliness of information;
- Understanding of the cost and benefits of data storage and usage;
- Breaking down of data silos and bringing them together dynamically to satisfy analytical requirements;
- Establishing good Governance, Risks, and Control (GRC).

Chapter 5
CEAF Governance

ABSTRACT

Governance, Risk Management, and Control (GRC) protect investments, provide transparency of decisions, and create accountability among government decision makers. The Collaborative Enterprise Architecture Framework (CEAF) requires an additional factor: making decisions based on government directions, and reducing the duplication of functionality among various government departments. These investments provide significantly higher value when they are protected by GRC, aligning investment with strategic direction. In the context of disruptive technologies, it is vital that these risks be identified quickly and handled effectively, as new technologies provide a wide gamut of options and expose the organisation to a suite of uncertainties, in terms of business and technology strategies and their execution. GRC brings together corporate governance, controls and reporting, and Enterprise Risk Management (ERM), in order to ensure compliance with rules and regulations. The components of GRC are defined as: 1) Governance, the overall management approach, and Controls to direct the organisation; 2) Risk management that supports governance, through which management identifies, analyses, and (where necessary) responds appropriately to risks; and 3) Compliance, conforming to stated Requirements, Standards, and Regulations.

DOI: 10.4018/978-1-5225-2407-6.ch005

INTRODUCTION

Disruptive technologies have significant business impact that must be identified quickly and handled effectively. The strategies and their execution are exposed to several unpredictable circumstances and risks, in the new spectrum of technological and business options. Including GRC in strategy planning will help identify risks and protect the systems. Additionally, GRC has a core task in maintaining compliance with legal, audit, and accounting requirements.

GOVERNANCE AND RISKS: A BALANCING ACT

The starting point for good governance is that it must be pragmatic. This means it should not only consider various organisational risks, but also balance them with the opportunities that accompany the project being assessed. Furthermore, risks need to be managed in such a way that they do not negatively impact quality, cost, and operational efficiency of the organisation. Accordingly, governance and risks are a balancing act to ensure achieving business objectives without sacrificing quality. Understanding business capabilities and limitations enhances GRC effectiveness and efficiency. This requires a good understanding of organisation-wide accepted business and technology strategies, and the way in which the organisation views opportunities and risks. Below are the key characteristics of a GRC framework:

- **Discipline:** Consistent criteria are used to assess multiple projects across an organisation, in terms of their business impact and outcomes. In the absence of an organisation-wide discipline, assessment of projects tends to be subjective and influenced by individual decision makers' personalities.
- **Transparency and Fairness:** Projects are assessed based on enterprise-wide principles and standards that are made part of the organisational framework. Here, current technologies create a need for extreme transparency, as the impact of technologies remains unknown for most business decision makers.
- **Independence:** Enterprise Architects (EA) must have independence so they can provide a range of realistic solutions based on organisational demands, and ensure that the organisation has the capabilities to incorporate and absorb the new technologies.

- **Accountability:** Architects and project managers are made accountable and responsible for documenting any deviations and exceptions in the architectural principles. This comes from the compliance aspect of GRC.

The above characteristics enable the GRC framework to provide stability to government-wide projects. Changes to GRC itself are permitted only when there is a change to the overall organisation, the responsibility and reporting model of the business, or the makeup of operating facilities. GRC is thus independent of management. It maintains the accountability and authority of managers, and defines their decisions and actions.

GRC protects business investments. By carefully mapping GRC to the CEAF, an organisation can ensure that projects get higher and more secure returns from investments, because GRC not only ensures compliance; it also is geared to ensuring value-for-money. Governance processes enhance common services, which, in turn, help identify risks up front. Once the risks are visible, effective controls to ameliorate those risks can be implemented. The purpose of the governance framework should be to support the fragmented and overlapping communities of interest within departments and agencies, to work toward a common goal of serving citizens in a cost-effective manner. The governance bodies also must validate the recommended tools and services, to provide optimal balance of internal and external information exchanges and services to constituents. The CEAF can enable and empower government employees and local communities by providing secured and contextualised information. The CEAF can assist in aggregating information across multiple agencies, jurisdictions, and information, to be available in a secure and personalised manner. The CEAF should assist in integrating a multi-departmental information exchange, and governance should make sure the information has not been accessed illegally or inappropriately. The CEAF adoption will need several governance forums or bodies with authority to make decisions for the development of services across the government. The following decision forums will be required for seamless adoption of CEAF across government departments and agencies:

- **Project Funding Governance:** CEAF adoption will require a framework to define the funding models for the common-services implementation. The governance framework will require the government to fund some of these services as foundation projects.

- **Data Governance:** The CEAF adoption will require a framework to define data governance across the whole of the government. This will require a common information-management framework implemented with a standard Business Classification Scheme for all information classification. The classification of information should apply to structured (stored in systems), unstructured, and semi-structured (such as emails, reports) information. CEAF services will use this classification to display it, based on security classification.
- **Services Governance:** The services governance will be difficult initially if the information management governance is not in place. Services governance needs a common framework to define services.
- **Security Governance:** This should be defined at all levels of information targeted for sharing. Citizen Services should have security embedded in the information. This may require encryption of information at the source, and decryption based only on the information requestor's security clearance.

The governing bodies will need authority to govern all IT functions in scope. For example, if the common services are in scope for the governing bodies, then the services governance authority's applicability to all IT functions related to the services also is in the scope of governance. The governing bodies must govern all technology, information, solution, and security changes. The objective of these forums should be to ensure that technology investment decisions are made transparently and on the grounds of best available information, including development of options, in the full enterprise context and considering the full lifecycle of the proposed technology. The governing bodies must require mandatory compliance with the CEAF and define a pragmatic process that includes exceptions granted for the content of the architecture. The governing bodies must have resources with right skills, decision-making authority, and ensured participation of key stakeholders.

Terms of reference for each governing body must be formalised. The terms of reference should include activities for reviewing strategic CEAF recommendations from the perspectives of delivery, infrastructure, data, security, vendors, and any relevant constraints.

The governing body should maintain necessary decision logs and registers (exemptions, architecture gaps) and the processes should be transparent and accountable. Governance is the overall management approach and the controls that direct the organisation. It requires an understanding of both the aspirations and the limitations of the organisation. The advent of disruptive technology requires even more governance than before, because of the multilayered data sources, which can be structured and unstructured. Risk Management supports governance through which management identifies, analyses, and, where necessary, responds appropriately to risks. Risks in the technology age are extremely dynamic—that is, they can come at any time, completely unanticipated. Compliance means conforming to stated Requirements, Standards, and Regulations. Due to the complexity of the volume of information that must be processed, compliance assumes greater importance than before. This is because compliance can percolate to many layers of business that could be responsible for the ultimate outcome.

Governance is usually top down. The priorities of government's operations, based on its strategies, can be approved and accepted by the organisation when it comes from the decision-makers and owners of the organisation. Effective governance is based on a body that comprises both operational and technical decision makers of the organisation. These groups synergise operations, strategy, and IT professionals to ensure that the relevant IT systems, services, and platforms support the organisation's outcomes. Assisting with these competencies is the enterprise architecture governance framework that ensures the architecture principles, standards, and guidelines are expressed along the lines of the organisational goals and strategies.

The GRC returns significant value when it is carefully mapped to business outcomes. This is so because apart from ensuring compliance, GRC is also geared toward ensuring the organisation gets what it has paid for. GRC benefits organisations provided they are controlled through governance processes, their risks are identified up front, and there are effective controls to handle the risks. Eventually, this is helpful in maintaining compliance with both external and internal legal, audit, and accounting requirements. This is vital to pave the path for sensible technology investments, which are themselves assuming significant importance and demanding great attention from decision makers in the era of information-driven technologies and businesses.

Governance Adoption and Maintenance

A nominated group must coordinate architectural governance. The governance forums must provide architectural, business, and change input to the leadership team on the basis of IT-investment alignment with organisational goals. It also assists in selecting optimal and pragmatic solutions for current business problems and governs the implementation. The Enterprise Architecture governance adoption must be a continuously reviewed and revised open plan that realigns efforts related to change activities. The architecture governing the systems and processes should evolve along with the business, as its demands change. Thus, the architecture should be dynamic and agile to meet business needs. The common objective of the governance forums must be to ensure that technology investment decisions are made efficiently and on the basis of the best available information, including development of options, in the full enterprise context, and considering the full life cycle of the proposed technology. These governance forums must enforce mandatory compliance with the Enterprise Architecture process framework. In many instances, overlap between the scopes of the governing bodies must be identified, and an escalation method defined as part of terms of reference.

Alignment

All aspects of the architecture must align with CEAF adoption strategies. As the Enterprise Architecture practice and content matures and becomes more closely aligned to strategic vision, IT operations and initiatives will directly increase business value and responsiveness. The following focus areas for Enterprise Architecture must be established:

- Articulate the value of Enterprise Architecture in a way that is relevant and applicable to individual operational areas, in order to embed the function rapidly and steer the levels of IT investment toward long-term competitive outcomes.
- Establish consistent Enterprise Architecture government departments to follow common principles, processes, and standards.
- Establish a transparent and effective means of assessing the trade off between local and Enterprise optimisation decisions, to assist in managing IT at an Enterprise level.
- Enhance business agility, with the goal of taking IT off the critical path to business change.
- Improve the speed and effectiveness of Enterprise Architecture engagements, including enhancing the commercial dimension of architecture decision making, and externalising the architecture perspective.
- Improve the return on investment of IT-project expenditure, including project and enterprise benefits.

Span of Organisation

Governance must affect all business areas across government departments. Difficult to implement, the scope of governance must be defined in key areas of service definition and infrastructure required to maintain services. It is important to encourage departments and agencies to agree and implement common standard principles across all IT investments. Initially these common standards should include the services and applications, processes, information repositories, and flows for all information and functionality that is new or will be changed in future to align with the agreed-upon strategic direction. Standards for all technical components, technical services, and infrastructure patterns or standard deployment models for typical solutions must be defined. The definition must include a framework for evaluating technical options within projects, to ensure the Enterprise context and the asset lifespan are transparently considered as part of upfront decision-making, and a framework for nonfunctional requirements. The governance function

Table 1. Artefacts for implementation of CEAF governance

Artefacts	Purpose
Architecture principles	The principles guide and constrain the choices made in the development and implementation of the framework. A number of principles must be defined for each CEAF domain. The definition of principles must be clear and adaptable within departments and agencies.
Design standards	Standards for services, technology, integration, and infrastructure implementation.
Reference Architecture	The Reference Architecture must be an authoritative source of information about a specific subject area that guides and restrains the occurrences of multiple architectures and solutions. The reference architecture must be defined with the target state and a roadmap in mind. The reference architecture must be pragmatic and adaptable to different maturity level of agencies and departments.
Ownerships	The following ownerships must be defined and maintained: • Information Owners • Information custodians • Policy Owner • Service Owner • System Owner
Governance term of reference	The terms of reference for all governance authorities must be approved by the senior executives and communicated to all stakeholders.
Decision logs	All decisions made by the governance authorities must be recorded, maintained, and published.
Governance prioritisation criteria	The governance forums should have key prioritisation criteria defined and socialised. The criteria must include alignment with target architecture, building priority capabilities, security requirements, reputation (loss), cost of the project, performance criteria, and government direction—political, legislative requirements, regulation.
Review cycle	The governance principles, standards, and patterns must be reviewed and updated to include new technology.

must govern all technology, information, solution, and security changes. It should not retroactively affect technologies, information, solutions, and business processes already installed, except when specifically identified in the strategic intents and roadmaps as necessary for integration. Compliance with the governance process must be mandatory. There may be exceptions granted for the content of the architecture; however, the primary purpose of the governance process is to ensure that business outcomes are met. Table 1 defines the artefacts that the governance authorities must create and maintain.

PROJECT FUNDING GOVERNANCE

GRC facilitates investment decisions, primarily based on cost-benefit analysis. However, other prioritisation mechanisms, such as regulatory demands, competition, and technology breakthroughs can also dictate investment decisions. Thus, a certain amount of Business Intelligence (BI) can be brought into making these decisions (Unhelkar & Tiwary, 2010). A traditional stage-gate process is based on a cost-benefit analysis. In this process, each project is assessed based on the project costs and benefits it can offer to the organisation. This method looks at each and every idea and initiative in isolation. While this has been the traditional and most popular approach to investment decisions, it does not encourage a holistic approach to a program of development for the entire organisation. The linear nature of this process leads to fragmented governance of projects. As such, it does not mitigate the risks of multiple simultaneous projects that may not be aware of each other. In such cases, GRC becomes a variation of a multigating process in which, at each gate, projects are assessed based on predefined milestones. This approach runs the risks of experienced project sponsors ticking the boxes to get projects through these loops. Apart from the risks of project conflicts, this can also result in building duplicate capabilities—a very real risk experienced across government agencies.

Linearly defined governance rules do not result in a cohesive whole that could be mapped to the strategic direction of the organisation. Government departments do not have access to unlimited funds to allocate to IT initiatives. Currently, ideas are selected or rejected based on individual business-case benefits. Change is required to fund initiatives for foundation projects. The government needs to have rules in place to assess and prioritise the suite of proposed foundation initiatives. The governance of the funding should change to align strategic goals with intended services the government plans to offer its constituents. This will require government directions, the services catalogue, and planned roadmaps to be available to all departments and divisions. The government should identify the project-governance process for funded foundation projects. An appropriate analytical prioritisation model enabling the government funding decision makers to make informed decisions as to which initiatives should receive funding must support the foundation funded services selection and governance. The key criteria for the funding should include verification of operational improvement across government departments. To approve a project, governance will need technical alignment with targeted government technical directions, and evidence that they will assist in improving benefits for future projects or support other initiatives, like foundation building blocks. The confidence in delivery must be road tested by the funding governance processes. Governance should assist decision makers in setting investment priorities. The funding governance should also get input from the other governance forums to make sure that ongoing and increasing requirements for security, accessibility, and agility are embedded in all IT systems, enabling the organisation to transform and change quickly to meet a more dynamic environment. The governance framework should assist decision makers in making better-informed decisions through the ability to quickly and accurately analyse information across all services expected from the government.

In order to ensure that funding is allocated to the highest-value initiatives, a consistent approach to the evaluation, comparison, and strategic ranking across competing IT initiatives and project proposals is critical. Appropriate enterprise-wide governance must be in place to address existing architectural and technical debts in a coordinated and efficient manner. The governance model should have a clear enterprise-wide focus to ensure that the Innovation Fund is applied according to the targeted business outcomes.

Bibliography

This book is been developed over number of years based on understanding the issues faced across various government departments. The collaborative enterprise architecture framework is based on the collaborative intelligence concepts. The CEAF framework is utilising some of learnings from my research and previous experience in private sector. This chapter provides a list of further reading material and also a number of references used throughout book. The CEAF implementation will require understanding of many foundation components discussed in this book and these references and further studies will assist in providing detailed implementation advice.

INFORMATION TECHNOLOGY STRATEGIES

The technology is changing drastically and most of areas discussed in the framework are going through a number of changes. The smart devices are providing information not previously available and will require organisation to rethink their communication, security and information management strategies.

- Balasubramanian, P., Kulatilaka, N., & Storck. (1998). *Managing information technology investments using a real-options approach*. School of Management, Boston University.
- Buytendijk & Oestreich. (2015). *Organizing for Big data through process and governance*. Gartner.
- Cruz-Cunha, M. M. (Ed.). (2010). *Social, managerial, and organizational dimensions of enterprise information systems*. Hershey, PA: IGI Global.
- Goel, A., Tiwary, A., & Schmidt, H. (2010). Approaches and initiatives to green IT strategy in business. In B. Unhelkar (Ed.), *Handbook*

of research on green ICT: Technical, methodological and social perspectives. Hershey, PA: IGI Global.

- Goel, A., Tiwary, A., & Schmidt, H. (2010). Green ICT and architectural frameworks. In B. Unhelkar (Ed.), *Handbook of research on green ICT: Technical, methodological and social perspectives*. Hershey, PA: IGI Global.
- Kleppmann, M. (2014). *Designing data-intensive applications*. Sebastopol, CA: O'Reilly.
- McKinsey Report. (2011). *Big data – The next frontier for innovation, competition and productivity*. McKinsey.
- Tiwary, A. (2010). *Collaborative intelligence*. Retrieved from http://alinement.net/component/content/article/50?Itemid=34
- Tiwary, A., & Unhelkar, B. (2011). Extending and applying business intelligence and customer strategies for green ICT. In B. Unhelkar (Ed.), *Handbook of research in green ICT: Technical, business and social perspectives*. Hershey, PA: IGI Global.
- Unhelkar, B., & Tiwary, A. (2010). Collaborative intelligence. *Cutter IT Journal, 23*(6).
- Unhelkar, B., Tiwary, A., & Ghanbary, A. (2009). Transitioning business processes to a collaborative business environment with mobility: An action research based on a service organization. In B. Unhelkar (Ed.), *Handbook of research in mobile business: Technical, methodological, and social perspectives* (2nd ed.). Hershey, PA: IGI Global.
- White, A., & Logan, D. (2015). *Governing the information governance*. Gartner.

ANALYTICS

Collaborations require a move away from only assessing internal data for the organization's performance to strategizing to incorporate external data (Big data including social and mobile media in various formats) relevant to organizational operations. Analytics area is seeing growth of new disciplines such as data scientist are becoming common across organisations. The volume of data is increasing exponentially and will make it difficult for any single organisation to have infrastructure and capacity to analyse. CEAF will assist organisations to develop a collaborative approach of predictive analytics.

- Abbott, D. (2014). *Applied predictive analytics: Principles and techniques for the professional data analyst*. John Wiley & Sons.
- Cielen, D., Meysman, A., & Ali, M. (2016). *Introducing data science: Big data, machine learning, and more, using Python tools*. Manning Publications.
- Collection of interviews. (2014). In *Data scientists at work*. APress.
- Giusti, A., & Ritter, G. (2012). *Classification and data mining*. Springer.
- Gorton, I., & Gracio, D. (2012). Data-intensive computing: Architectures, algorithms, and applications. Cambridge University Press.
- Manoochehri, M. (2013). *Data just right: Introduction to large-scale data & analytics*. Reading, MA: Addison Wesley.
- Meyer, M., & Fisher, D. (2016). *Making sense of data: Designing effective visualizations*. Sebastopol, CA: O'Reilly.
- Morabito, V. (2015). *Big data and analytics: Strategic and organizational impacts*. Springer.
- Pascale, Z. (2013). *Tools for collaborative decision-making*. Hoboken, NJ: John Wiley & Sons.
- Syvajarvi, M., & Stenvall, J. (Eds.). (2010). *Data mining in public and private sectors: Organizational and government applications*. Hershey, PA: IGI Global.

NETWORK SECURITY

- Campisi, P. (2013). *Security and privacy in biometrics*. Springer.
- Cao, J., & Zhang, C. (2014). *Seamless and secure communications over heterogeneous wireless networks*. Springer.
- Craig, T., & Ludloff, M. (2011). *Privacy and big data*. Sebastopol, CA: O'Reilly.
- Effelsberg, W., & Steinmetz, R. (2013). *Benchmarking peer-to-peer systems: Understanding quality of service in large-scale distributed systems*. Springer.
- Leeuw, E., & Fischer-Hübner, S. (Eds.). (2010). *Policies and research in identity management: Second IFIP WG 11.6 working conference*. Springer.
- Pearson, S., & Yee, G. (2012). *Privacy and security for cloud computing*. Springer.

- Serpanos, D., & Wolf, T. (2011). *Architecture of network systems*. Morgan Kauffman.
- Shen, X., You, H., Buford, J., & Akon, M. (Eds.). (2009). *Handbook of peer-to-peer networking*. Springer.
- Taylor, I., & Harrison, A. (2008). *From P2P and grids to services on the web: Evolving distributed communities*. Springer.
- Vacca, J. (2014). *Network and system security* (2nd ed.). Syngress Publishing.

COLLABORATIVE WORKING

- Archer, D., & Cameron, A. (2009). *Collaborative leadership: How to succeed in an interconnected world*. Routledge.
- Bente, S., & Bombosch, U. (2012). *Collaborative enterprise architecture: Enriching EA with lean, agile, and enterprise 2.0 practices*. Morgan Kaufmann.
- Bratton, W., & Tumin, Z. (2012). *Collaborate or perish! Reaching across boundaries in a networked world*. Crown.
- Cao, M., & Zhang, O. (2012). *Supply chain collaboration: Roles of interorganizational systems, trust, and collaborative culture*. Springer.
- Chang, W., Abu-Amara, H., & Sanford, J. (2010). *Transforming enterprise cloud services*. Springer.
- Familiar, B. (2015). *Microservices, IoT and Azure: Leveraging DevOps and microservice architecture to deliver SaaS solutions*. Apress.
- Garson, G., & Khosrow-Pour, M. (Eds.). (2008). *Handbook of research on public information technology*. Hershey, PA: IGI Global.
- Immordino, K. (2009). *Organizational assessment and improvement in the public sector*. CRC Press.
- Kock, N. (2007). *E-collaboration in modern organizations: Initiating and managing distributed projects*. Hershey, PA: IGI Global.
- Luis, M., & Camarinha-Matos, P. W. (Eds.). (2008). *Pervasive collaborative networks: IFIP TC 5 WG 5.5 ninth working conference on virtual enterprises*. Springer.
- Sanker, D. (2012). *Collaborate: The art of we*. San Francisco, CA: Jossey-Bass.
- Van Bommel, P. (2004). *Transformation of knowledge, information and data: Theory and applications*. Hershey, PA: IGI Global.

- Xhafa, F., & Bessis, N. (2013). *Inter-cooperative collective intelligence: Techniques and applications*. Springer.
- Zhou, H. (2012). *The internet of things in the cloud: A middleware perspective*. Boca Raton, FL: CRC Press.

DISRUPTIVE TECHNOLOGY

- Cook, N. (2008). *Enterprise 2.0*. Ashgate.
- Heisterberg, R., & Verma, A. (2014). *Creating business agility: How convergence of cloud, social, mobile, video, and big data enables competitive advantage*. Hoboken, NJ: John Wiley & Sons.
- Jeston, J., & Nelis, J. (2008). *Business process management*. Routledge.
- Kavis, M. J. (2012). *Architecting the cloud: Design decisions for cloud computing service models (SaaS, PaaS, and IaaS)*. Hoboken, NJ: John Wiley & Sons.
- Mirabito, M., & Morgenstern, B. (2004). *The new communications technologies: Applications, policy, and impact* (5th ed.). Focal Press.
- Resmini, A., & Rosati, L. (2011). *Pervasive information architecture: Designing cross-channel user experiences*. Morgan and Claypool Publishers.
- Vom Brocke, J., & Rosemann, M. (Eds.). (2014). *Handbook on business process management 2: Strategic alignment, governance, people and culture*. Springer.

E-GOVERNMENT

- Anttiroiko, A., & Malkia, M. (Eds.). (2006). *Encyclopedia of digital government*. Hershey, PA: IGI Global.
- Assar, S., Boughzala, I., & Boydens, I. (2010). *Practical studies in e-government: Best practices from around the world*. Springer.
- Botsman, R., & Rogers, R. (2011). *What's mine is yours: The rise of collaborative consumption*. Collins.
- Curts, J. J., & Campbell, D. E. (2002). *Building a global information assurance program*. Auerbach Publications.
- George, J. A., & Rodger, J. A. (2010). *Smart data: Enterprise performance optimization strategy*. Hoboken, NJ: John Wiley & Sons.

- Gingrich, J. (2003). *Managing IT in government, business & communities*. IRM Press.
- Gronlund, A. (2002). *Electronic government: Design, applications and management*. Hershey, PA: IGI Global.
- Heeks, R. (2005). *Implementing and managing egovernment: An international text*. Thousand Oaks, CA: Sage Publications.
- Kushch, I. (2007). *Mobile government: An emerging direction in e-government*. Hershey, PA: IGI Global.
- Lathrop, D., & Ruma, L. (2010). *Open government: Collaboration, transparency, and participation in practice*. Sebastopol, CA: O'Reilly.
- Mälkiä, M., Anttiroiko, A., & Savolainen, A. (2003). *Etransformation in governance: New directions in government and politics*. Hershey, PA: IGI Global.
- McIver, W., Jr., & Elmagarmid, A. K. (2002). *Advances in digital government*. Springer.
- National Research Council. (2003). *Government data centers: Meeting increasing demands*. Washington, DC: National Academy Press.
- Norris, D. F. (2007). *E-government research: Policy and management*. Hershey, PA: IGI Global.
- Noveck, B. E (2009). *Wiki government: How technology can make government better, democracy stronger, and citizens more powerful*. Brookings Institution Press.
- West, D. M. (2005). *Digital government: Technology and public sector performance*. Princeton, NJ: Princeton Press.
- Wood, D. (2011). *Linking government data*. Springer.

MACHINE LEARNING

- Babuska, R., & Groen, F. (2010). *Interactive collaborative information systems*. Springer.
- Morris, M. R., & Teevan, J. (2009). *Collaborative search: Designing systems for a spectrum of collaborative styles*. Morgan and Claypool Publishers.
- Stahl, G. (2006). *Group cognition: Computer support for building collaborative knowledge*. Cambridge, MA: MIT Press.
- Sukhtankar, G., Goldman, G., Geib, C., Pynadath, P. V., & Riji, H. H. (2014). *Plan, activity, and intent recognition: Theory and practice*. Morgan Kaufmann.

- Wang, W., & Tsai, J. J. (2011). *Collaborative design in virtual environments*. Springer.

ENTERPRISE ARCHITECTURE

- Bente, S., & Bombosch, U. (2012). *Collaborative enterprise architecture: Enriching EA with lean, agile, and enterprise 2.0 practices*. Morgan Kaufmann.
- Bloomberg, J. (2013). *The agile architecture revolution: How cloud computing, REST-based SOA, and mobile computing are changing enterprise IT*. Hoboken, NJ: John Wiley & Sons.
- Duggan, D. (2012). *Enterprise software architecture and design: Entities, services, and resources*. Hoboken, NJ: John Wiley & Sons.
- Luisi, J. (2014). *Pragmatic enterprise architecture: Strategies to transform information systems in the era of big data*. Morgan Kaufmann.
- Schekkerman, J. (2013). *How to survive in the jungle of enterprise architecture frameworks: Creating or choosing an enterprise architecture framework*. Trafford Publishing.
- Wood, D. (2010). *Linking enterprise data*. Springer.

EXTRA READING ON ROI

- Poniatowski, M. (2009). *Foundations of green IT: Consolidation, virtualization, efficiency, and ROI in the data center*. Prentice Hall.
- Wise, L. (2012). *Using open source platforms for business intelligence: Avoid pitfalls and maximize ROI*. Morgan Kaufmann.

KNOWLEDGE MANAGEMENT

- Eardley, A., & Uden, A. (2010). *Innovative knowledge management: Concepts for organizational creativity and collaborative design*. Hershey, PA: IGI Global.
- Jennex, M. (2005). *Case studies in knowledge management*. Hershey, PA: IGI Global.
- Kocaturk, T., & Medjdoub, B. (2011). *Distributed intelligence in design*. Hoboken, NJ: John Wiley & Sons.

- McNabb, D. E. (2006). *Knowledge management in the public sector: A blueprint for innovation in government*. M.E. Sharpe.
- Yoong, P. (2009). *Leadership in the digital enterprise: Issues and challenges*. Business Science.

GENERAL MANAGEMENT

- Berson, A., & Dubov, L. (2007). *Master data management and customer data integration for a global enterprise*. McGraw-Hill.
- Biafore, B. (2011). *Successful project management: Applying best practices and real-world techniques with Microsoft project*. Microsoft Press.
- Blanchard, O. (2011). *Social media ROI: Managing and measuring social media efforts in your organization*. Que.
- Doan, A., & Halevy, A. (2012). *Principles of data integration*. Morgan Kaufmann.
- George, J. A., & Rodger, J. A. (2010). *Smart data: Enterprise performance optimization strategy*. Hoboken, NJ: John Wiley & Sons.
- Han, K. J., & Choi, B. (2013). *High performance cloud auditing and applications*. Springer.
- Hay, D. C. (2002). *Requirements analysis: From business views to architecture*. Prentice Hall.
- McKnight, W. (2013). *Information management: Strategies for gaining a competitive advantage with data*. Morgan Kaufmann.
- Naroff, J. L., & Scherer, R. (2014). *Big picture economics: How to navigate the new global economy*. Hoboken, NJ: John Wiley & Sons.
- Orr, L. M., & Orr, D. J. (2014). *Eliminating waste in business: Run lean, boost profitability*. Apress.
- Phillips, J. J., & Schmidt, L. (2011). *The leadership scorecard*. Routledge.
- Smith, P. (2012). *Lead with a story: A guide to crafting business narratives that captivate, convince, and inspire*. AMACOM.
- Solingen, R. V., & Berghout, E. (1999). *Goal/question/metric method*. McGraw-Hill.
- Stephens, R. (2015). *Beginning software engineering*. Wrox Press.
- Thamhain, H. J. (2014). *Managing technology-based projects: Tools, techniques, people and business processes*. Hoboken, NJ: John Wiley & Sons.

- Verzuh, E. (2013). *The portable MBA in project management*. Hoboken, NJ: John Wiley & Sons.

SERVICE-ORIENTED ARCHITECTURE (SOA)

- Bell, M. (2010). *SOA modelling patterns for service-oriented discovery and analysis*. Hoboken, NJ: John Wiley & Sons.
- Berg, M., & Bieberstein, N. (2007). *SOA for profit: A manager's guide to success with service-oriented architecture*. IBM Press.
- Biske, T. (2008). *SOA governance*. Packt Publishing.
- Erl, T., & Bennett, S. G. (2011). *SOA governance: Governing shared services on-premise and in the cloud*. Prentice Hall.
- Garzás, J., & Piattini, M. (2006). *Object-oriented design knowledge: Principles, heuristics and best practices*. Hershey, PA: IGI Global.
- Isaacson, C. (2009). *Software pipelines and SOA: Releasing the power of multi-core processing*. Reading, MA: Addison Wesley.
- Krendzel, A. V. (Ed.). (2012). *Wireless mesh networks – Efficient link scheduling, channel assignment and network planning strategies*. InTech.
- Linthicum, D. S. (2009). *Cloud computing and SOA convergence in your enterprise: A step-by-step guide*. Reading, MA: Addison Wesley.
- Marks, E. A., & Bell, M. (2006). *Service-oriented architecture (SOA): A planning and implementation guide for business and technology*. Hoboken, NJ: John Wiley & Sons.
- Rotem-Gal-Oz, A. (2012). *SOA patterns*. Manning Publications.
- Sun, R. (2005). *Cognition and multi-agent interaction: From cognitive modeling to social simulation*. Cambridge, UK: Cambridge University Press.
- Sweeney, R. (2010). *Achieving service-oriented architecture: Applying an enterprise architecture approach*. Hoboken, NJ: John Wiley & Sons.

AGILE

- Alaybeyi, B., Tully, J., & Jones, N. (2016, May 9). *Build your blueprint for the internet of things, based on five architectural components*. Gartner.

- Bloomberg, J. (2013). *The agile architecture revolution: How cloud computing, REST-based SOA, and mobile computing are changing enterprise IT*. Hoboken, NJ: John Wiley & Sons.
- Bregman, A. C. (2017, Jan 4). Execution is a people problem, not a strategy problem. *Harvard Business Review*.
- Coleman, J. (2017, Jan 4). The best strategic leaders balance agility and consistency. *Harvard Business Review*.
- Davenport, T. H. (2007, Dec 6). Avoid the extremes. *Harvard Business Review*.
- Edmondson, A. C. (2011, Apr). Strategies for learning from failure. *Harvard Business Review*.
- Favaro, K. (2015, March 31). Defining strategy, implementation, and execution. *Harvard Business Review*.
- Gorton, I., & Gracio, D. K. (2012). *Data-intensive computing: Architectures, algorithms, and applications*. Cambridge, UK: Cambridge University Press.
- Hammarberg, M., & Sunden, J. (2014). *Kanban in action*. Manning Publications.
- Kim, W. C., & Mauborgne, R. (2015, Feb 5). Closing the gap between blue ocean strategy and execution. *Harvard Business Review*.
- Leffingwell, D. (2011). *Agile software requirements: Lean requirements practices for teams, programs, and the enterprise*. Reading, MA: Addison Wesley.
- Leinwand, P., Mainardi, C., & Kleiner, A. (2015, Dec 30). Only 8 percent of leaders are good at both strategy and execution. *Harvard Business Review*.
- Martin, R. L. (2015, Sep 15). Why talking about strategy "execution" is still dangerous. *Harvard Business Review*.
- Meyer, B. (2014). *Agile! The good, the hype and the ugly*. Springer.
- Park, J., & Hwang, J. (2003). Role-based access control for collaborative enterprise in peer-to-peer computing environments. *SACMAT '03 Proceedings of the Eighth ACM Symposium on Access Control Models and Technologies*.
- Stellman, A., & Greene, J. (2014). *Learning agile: Understanding Scrum, XP, Lean, and Kanban*. Sebastopol, CA: O'Reilly.
- Sull, D., Homkes, R., & Sull, C. (2015, Mar). Why strategy execution unravels – And what to do about it. *Harvard Business Review*.
- Tapadinhas, J. (2016, Apr 12). *Select the right architecture model for your modern BI and analytics platform*. Gartner.

- Wiegers, K., & Beatty, J. (2013). *Software requirements* (3rd ed.). Microsoft Press.
- Wysocki, R. K. (2013). *Effective project management: Traditional, agile, extreme*. Hoboken, NJ: John Wiley & Sons.

Related Readings

To continue IGI Global's long-standing tradition of advancing innovation through emerging research, please find below a compiled list of recommended IGI Global book chapters and journal articles in the areas of enterprise architecture, cloud computing, and internet security. These related readings will provide additional information and guidance to further enrich your knowledge and assist you with your own research.

Adeel, M. (2016). Big Data Virtualization and Visualization: On the Cloud. In R. Kannan, R. Rasool, H. Jin, & S. Balasundaram (Eds.), *Managing and Processing Big Data in Cloud Computing* (pp. 168–184). Hershey, PA: IGI Global. doi:10.4018/978-1-4666-9767-6.ch012

Adhikari, M., Das, A., & Mukherjee, A. (2016). Utility Computing and Its Utilization. In G. Deka, G. Siddesh, K. Srinivasa, & L. Patnaik (Eds.), *Emerging Research Surrounding Power Consumption and Performance Issues in Utility Computing* (pp. 1–21). Hershey, PA: IGI Global. doi:10.4018/978-1-4666-8853-7.ch001

Adhikari, M., & Kar, S. (2016). Advanced Topics GPU Programming and CUDA Architecture. In G. Deka, G. Siddesh, K. Srinivasa, & L. Patnaik (Eds.), *Emerging Research Surrounding Power Consumption and Performance Issues in Utility Computing* (pp. 175–203). Hershey, PA: IGI Global. doi:10.4018/978-1-4666-8853-7.ch008

Adhikari, M., & Roy, D. (2016). Green Computing. In G. Deka, G. Siddesh, K. Srinivasa, & L. Patnaik (Eds.), *Emerging Research Surrounding Power Consumption and Performance Issues in Utility Computing* (pp. 84–108). Hershey, PA: IGI Global. doi:10.4018/978-1-4666-8853-7.ch005

Ahmad, F. (2016). Big Data Virtualization and Visualization on Cloud. In R. Kannan, R. Rasool, H. Jin, & S. Balasundaram (Eds.), *Managing and Processing Big Data in Cloud Computing* (pp. 145–155). Hershey, PA: IGI Global. doi:10.4018/978-1-4666-9767-6.ch010

Ahmad, K., Kumar, G., Wahid, A., & Kirmani, M. M. (2016). Software Performance Estimate using Fuzzy Based Backpropagation Learning. In G. Deka, G. Siddesh, K. Srinivasa, & L. Patnaik (Eds.), *Emerging Research Surrounding Power Consumption and Performance Issues in Utility Computing* (pp. 320–344). Hershey, PA: IGI Global. doi:10.4018/978-1-4666-8853-7.ch016

Al-Begain, K., Zak, M., Alosaimi, W., & Turyagyenda, C. (2015). Security of the Cloud. In S. Bagchi (Ed.), *Emerging Research in Cloud Distributed Computing Systems* (pp. 363–404). Hershey, PA: IGI Global. doi:10.4018/978-1-4666-8213-9.ch012

Alling, A., Powers, N. R., & Soyata, T. (2016). Face Recognition: A Tutorial on Computational Aspects. In G. Deka, G. Siddesh, K. Srinivasa, & L. Patnaik (Eds.), *Emerging Research Surrounding Power Consumption and Performance Issues in Utility Computing* (pp. 405–425). Hershey, PA: IGI Global. doi:10.4018/978-1-4666-8853-7.ch020

Alohali, B. (2017). Detection Protocol of Possible Crime Scenes Using Internet of Things (IoT). In M. Moore (Ed.), *Cybersecurity Breaches and Issues Surrounding Online Threat Protection* (pp. 175–196). Hershey, PA: IGI Global. doi:10.4018/978-1-5225-1941-6.ch008

Alotaibi, R., Ramachandran, M., Kor, A., & Hosseinian-Far, A. (2016). Adoption of Social Media as Communication Channels in Government Agencies. In Z. Mahmood (Ed.), *Cloud Computing Technologies for Connected Government* (pp. 39–73). Hershey, PA: IGI Global. doi:10.4018/978-1-4666-8629-8.ch003

Ammari, H. M., Shaout, A., & Mustapha, F. (2017). Sensing Coverage in Three-Dimensional Space: A Survey. In N. Ray & A. Turuk (Eds.), *Handbook of Research on Advanced Wireless Sensor Network Applications, Protocols, and Architectures* (pp. 1–28). Hershey, PA: IGI Global. doi:10.4018/978-1-5225-0486-3.ch001

Anshari, M., & Almunawar, M. N. (2016). E-Government Initiatives through Cloud Computing: Empowering Citizens. In Z. Mahmood (Ed.), *Cloud Computing Technologies for Connected Government* (pp. 74–92). Hershey, PA: IGI Global. doi:10.4018/978-1-4666-8629-8.ch004

Anwar, H., Shibli, M. A., & Habiba, U. (2016). An Extensible Identity Management Framework for Cloud-Based E-Government Systems. In Z. Mahmood (Ed.), *Cloud Computing Technologies for Connected Government* (pp. 163–187). Hershey, PA: IGI Global. doi:10.4018/978-1-4666-8629-8.ch007

Armstrong, S., & Yampolskiy, R. V. (2017). Security Solutions for Intelligent and Complex Systems. In M. Dawson, M. Eltayeb, & M. Omar (Eds.), *Security Solutions for Hyperconnectivity and the Internet of Things* (pp. 37–88). Hershey, PA: IGI Global. doi:10.4018/978-1-5225-0741-3.ch003

Arulogun, T., AlSa'deh, A., & Meinel, C. (2014). Mobile IPv6: Mobility Management and Security Aspects. In A. Ruiz-Martinez, R. Marin-Lopez, & F. Pereniguez-Garcia (Eds.), *Architectures and Protocols for Secure Information Technology Infrastructures* (pp. 71–101). Hershey, PA: IGI Global. doi:10.4018/978-1-4666-4514-1.ch003

Ashraf, U., Rizvi, S. S., & Azeem, M. F. (2016). Performance Evaluation of Routing Metrics in Wireless Multi-Hop Networks. In R. Kannan, R. Rasool, H. Jin, & S. Balasundaram (Eds.), *Managing and Processing Big Data in Cloud Computing* (pp. 85–104). Hershey, PA: IGI Global. doi:10.4018/978-1-4666-9767-6.ch006

Atli, D. (2017). Cybercrimes via Virtual Currencies in International Business. In M. Moore (Ed.), *Cybersecurity Breaches and Issues Surrounding Online Threat Protection* (pp. 121–143). Hershey, PA: IGI Global. doi:10.4018/978-1-5225-1941-6.ch006

Bamrara, A. (2017). Identifying and Analyzing the Latent Cyber Threats in Developing Economies. In M. Moore (Ed.), *Cybersecurity Breaches and Issues Surrounding Online Threat Protection* (pp. 74–94). Hershey, PA: IGI Global. doi:10.4018/978-1-5225-1941-6.ch004

Bandopadhaya, S., & Roy, J. S. (2017). Spectral Efficiency in Wireless Networks through MIMO-OFDM System. In N. Ray & A. Turuk (Eds.), *Handbook of Research on Advanced Wireless Sensor Network Applications, Protocols, and Architectures* (pp. 249–277). Hershey, PA: IGI Global. doi:10.4018/978-1-5225-0486-3.ch010

Benadda, M., Bouamrane, K., & Belalem, G. (2017). How to Manage Persons Taken Malaise at the Steering Wheel Using HAaaS in a Vehicular Cloud Computing Environment. *International Journal of Ambient Computing and Intelligence*, *8*(2), 70–87. doi:10.4018/IJACI.2017040105

Bhadoria, R. S. (2016). Performance of Enterprise Architecture in Utility Computing. In G. Deka, G. Siddesh, K. Srinivasa, & L. Patnaik (Eds.), *Emerging Research Surrounding Power Consumption and Performance Issues in Utility Computing* (pp. 44–68). Hershey, PA: IGI Global. doi:10.4018/978-1-4666-8853-7.ch003

Bhadoria, R. S., & Patil, C. (2016). Adaptive Mobile Architecture with Utility Computing. In G. Deka, G. Siddesh, K. Srinivasa, & L. Patnaik (Eds.), *Emerging Research Surrounding Power Consumption and Performance Issues in Utility Computing* (pp. 386–404). Hershey, PA: IGI Global. doi:10.4018/978-1-4666-8853-7.ch019

Bhardwaj, A. (2017). Solutions for Securing End User Data over the Cloud Deployed Applications. In M. Moore (Ed.), *Cybersecurity Breaches and Issues Surrounding Online Threat Protection* (pp. 198–218). Hershey, PA: IGI Global. doi:10.4018/978-1-5225-1941-6.ch009

Bhargavi, K., & Babu, B. S. (2016). GPU Computation and Platforms. In G. Deka, G. Siddesh, K. Srinivasa, & L. Patnaik (Eds.), *Emerging Research Surrounding Power Consumption and Performance Issues in Utility Computing* (pp. 136–174). Hershey, PA: IGI Global. doi:10.4018/978-1-4666-8853-7.ch007

Cano, J., & Hernández, R. (2017). Managing Software Architecture in Domains of Security-Critical Systems: Multifaceted Collaborative eGovernment Projects. In S. Zoughbi (Ed.), *Securing Government Information and Data in Developing Countries* (pp. 1–26). Hershey, PA: IGI Global. doi:10.4018/978-1-5225-1703-0.ch001

Cardenas-Haro, J. A., & Dawson, M. (2017). Tails Linux Operating System: The Amnesiac Incognito System in Times of High Surveillance, Its Security Flaws, Limitations, and Strengths in the Fight for Democracy. In M. Dawson, M. Eltayeb, & M. Omar (Eds.), *Security Solutions for Hyperconnectivity and the Internet of Things* (pp. 260–271). Hershey, PA: IGI Global. doi:10.4018/978-1-5225-0741-3.ch010

Cardoso, A., Moreira, F., & Simões, P. (2016). A Support Framework for the Migration of E-Government Services to the Cloud. In Z. Mahmood (Ed.), *Cloud Computing Technologies for Connected Government* (pp. 124–162). Hershey, PA: IGI Global. doi:10.4018/978-1-4666-8629-8.ch006

Chen, C. K., & Almunawar, M. N. (2016). Cost Benefits of Cloud Computing for Connected Government. In Z. Mahmood (Ed.), *Cloud Computing Technologies for Connected Government* (pp. 345–368). Hershey, PA: IGI Global. doi:10.4018/978-1-4666-8629-8.ch014

Copil, G., Moldovan, D., Le, H. D., Truong, H., Dustdar, S., Sofokleous, C., & Xing, W. et al. (2015). On Controlling Elasticity of Cloud Applications in CELAR. In S. Bagchi (Ed.), *Emerging Research in Cloud Distributed Computing Systems* (pp. 222–252). Hershey, PA: IGI Global. doi:10.4018/978-1-4666-8213-9.ch007

Cordeschi, N., Shojafar, M., Amendola, D., & Baccarelli, E. (2015). Energy-Saving QoS Resource Management of Virtualized Networked Data Centers for Big Data Stream Computing. In S. Bagchi (Ed.), *Emerging Research in Cloud Distributed Computing Systems* (pp. 122–155). Hershey, PA: IGI Global. doi:10.4018/978-1-4666-8213-9.ch004

Dahal, S., & Ray, N. K. (2017). Intrusion Detection in MANET for Network Layer. In N. Ray & A. Turuk (Eds.), *Handbook of Research on Advanced Wireless Sensor Network Applications, Protocols, and Architectures* (pp. 326–352). Hershey, PA: IGI Global. doi:10.4018/978-1-5225-0486-3.ch013

Dale, M. (2016). Putting Implementation into Enterprise Architecture Research. *International Journal of Enterprise Information Systems, 12*(2), 14–25. doi:10.4018/IJEIS.2016040102

Das, P. K. (2016). Comparative Study on XEN, KVM, VSphere, and Hyper-V. In G. Deka, G. Siddesh, K. Srinivasa, & L. Patnaik (Eds.), *Emerging Research Surrounding Power Consumption and Performance Issues in Utility Computing* (pp. 233–261). Hershey, PA: IGI Global. doi:10.4018/978-1-4666-8853-7.ch011

Das, P. K., & Deka, G. C. (2016). History and Evolution of GPU Architecture. In G. Deka, G. Siddesh, K. Srinivasa, & L. Patnaik (Eds.), *Emerging Research Surrounding Power Consumption and Performance Issues in Utility Computing* (pp. 109–135). Hershey, PA: IGI Global. doi:10.4018/978-1-4666-8853-7.ch006

Dawson, M. (2017). Exploring Secure Computing for the Internet of Things, Internet of Everything, Web of Things, and Hyperconnectivity. In M. Dawson, M. Eltayeb, & M. Omar (Eds.), *Security Solutions for Hyperconnectivity and the Internet of Things* (pp. 1–12). Hershey, PA: IGI Global. doi:10.4018/978-1-5225-0741-3.ch001

Delgado, J. C. (2015). Distributed Interoperability in Heterogeneous Cloud Systems. In S. Bagchi (Ed.), *Emerging Research in Cloud Distributed Computing Systems* (pp. 1–40). Hershey, PA: IGI Global. doi:10.4018/978-1-4666-8213-9.ch001

Dokhanchi, A., & Nazemi, E. (2015). BISC: A Framework for Aligning Business Intelligence with Corporate Strategies Based on Enterprise Architecture Framework. *International Journal of Enterprise Information Systems*, *11*(2), 90–106. doi:10.4018/IJEIS.2015040105

Draper-Gil, G., Ferrer-Gomila, J., Hinarejos, M. F., & Tauber, A. (2014). Towards a Certified Electronic Mail System. In A. Ruiz-Martinez, R. Marin-Lopez, & F. Pereniguez-Garcia (Eds.), *Architectures and Protocols for Secure Information Technology Infrastructures* (pp. 46–70). Hershey, PA: IGI Global. doi:10.4018/978-1-4666-4514-1.ch002

Easton, J., & Parmar, R. (2017). Navigating Your Way to the Hybrid Cloud. In J. Chen, Y. Zhang, & R. Gottschalk (Eds.), *Handbook of Research on End-to-End Cloud Computing Architecture Design* (pp. 15–38). Hershey, PA: IGI Global. doi:10.4018/978-1-5225-0759-8.ch002

Egwutuoha, I. P., & Chen, S. (2017). Cost of Using Cloud Computing: HaaS vs. IaaS. In J. Chen, Y. Zhang, & R. Gottschalk (Eds.), *Handbook of Research on End-to-End Cloud Computing Architecture Design* (pp. 455–472). Hershey, PA: IGI Global. doi:10.4018/978-1-5225-0759-8.ch018

Ehrhardt, R. (2017). Cloud Build Methodology. In J. Chen, Y. Zhang, & R. Gottschalk (Eds.), *Handbook of Research on End-to-End Cloud Computing Architecture Design* (pp. 105–129). Hershey, PA: IGI Global. doi:10.4018/978-1-5225-0759-8.ch006

Eigenbrode, S., & Nassar, S. (2017). Design and Implementation of Service Management in DevOps Enabled Cloud Computing Models. In J. Chen, Y. Zhang, & R. Gottschalk (Eds.), *Handbook of Research on End-to-End Cloud Computing Architecture Design* (pp. 326–347). Hershey, PA: IGI Global. doi:10.4018/978-1-5225-0759-8.ch014

El Alami, H., & Najid, A. (2017). (SET) Smart Energy Management and Throughput Maximization: A New Routing Protocol for WSNs. In K. Munir (Ed.), *Security Management in Mobile Cloud Computing* (pp. 1–28). Hershey, PA: IGI Global. doi:10.4018/978-1-5225-0602-7.ch001

El Moussaid, N., & Toumanari, A. (2017). A Cloud Intrusion Detection Based on Classification of Activities and Mobile Agent. In K. Munir (Ed.), *Security Management in Mobile Cloud Computing* (pp. 29–42). Hershey, PA: IGI Global. doi:10.4018/978-1-5225-0602-7.ch002

Elkabbany, G. F., & Rasslan, M. (2017). Security Issues in Distributed Computing System Models. In M. Dawson, M. Eltayeb, & M. Omar (Eds.), *Security Solutions for Hyperconnectivity and the Internet of Things* (pp. 211–259). Hershey, PA: IGI Global. doi:10.4018/978-1-5225-0741-3.ch009

Elkhodr, M., Shahrestani, S., & Cheung, H. (2017). Internet of Things Research Challenges. In M. Dawson, M. Eltayeb, & M. Omar (Eds.), *Security Solutions for Hyperconnectivity and the Internet of Things* (pp. 13–36). Hershey, PA: IGI Global. doi:10.4018/978-1-5225-0741-3.ch002

Eltayeb, M. (2017). Privacy and Security. In M. Dawson, M. Eltayeb, & M. Omar (Eds.), *Security Solutions for Hyperconnectivity and the Internet of Things* (pp. 89–112). Hershey, PA: IGI Global. doi:10.4018/978-1-5225-0741-3.ch004

Emeakaroha, V. C., Netto, M. A., Brandic, I., & De Rose, C. A. (2015). Application-Level Monitoring and SLA Violation Detection for Multi-Tenant Cloud Services. In S. Bagchi (Ed.), *Emerging Research in Cloud Distributed Computing Systems* (pp. 157–186). Hershey, PA: IGI Global. doi:10.4018/978-1-4666-8213-9.ch005

Erdenebold, T. (2017). A Smart Government Framework for Mobile Application Services in Mongolia. In S. Zoughbi (Ed.), *Securing Government Information and Data in Developing Countries* (pp. 90–103). Hershey, PA: IGI Global. doi:10.4018/978-1-5225-1703-0.ch005

Erturk, E. (2017). Cloud Computing and Cybersecurity Issues Facing Local Enterprises. In M. Moore (Ed.), *Cybersecurity Breaches and Issues Surrounding Online Threat Protection* (pp. 219–247). Hershey, PA: IGI Global. doi:10.4018/978-1-5225-1941-6.ch010

Fatima, K., & Majeed, H. (2016). Texture-Based Evolutionary Method for Cancer Classification in Histopathology. In R. Kannan, R. Rasool, H. Jin, & S. Balasundaram (Eds.), *Managing and Processing Big Data in Cloud Computing* (pp. 55–69). Hershey, PA: IGI Global. doi:10.4018/978-1-4666-9767-6.ch004

Ferdaus, M. H., Murshed, M., Calheiros, R. N., & Buyya, R. (2015). Network-Aware Virtual Machine Placement and Migration in Cloud Data Centers. In S. Bagchi (Ed.), *Emerging Research in Cloud Distributed Computing Systems* (pp. 42–91). Hershey, PA: IGI Global. doi:10.4018/978-1-4666-8213-9.ch002

Ferreira da Silva, R., Glatard, T., & Desprez, F. (2015). Self-Management of Operational Issues for Grid Computing: The Case of the Virtual Imaging Platform. In S. Bagchi (Ed.), *Emerging Research in Cloud Distributed Computing Systems* (pp. 187–221). Hershey, PA: IGI Global. doi:10.4018/978-1-4666-8213-9.ch006

Fritscher, B., & Pigneur, Y. (2015). A Visual Approach to Business IT Alignment between Business Model and Enterprise Architecture. *International Journal of Information System Modeling and Design*, *6*(1), 1–23. doi:10.4018/ijismd.2015010101

Gahlawat, M., & Sharma, P. (2016). Green, Energy-Efficient Computing and Sustainability Issues in Cloud. In R. Kannan, R. Rasool, H. Jin, & S. Balasundaram (Eds.), *Managing and Processing Big Data in Cloud Computing* (pp. 206–217). Hershey, PA: IGI Global. doi:10.4018/978-1-4666-9767-6.ch014

Ghany, K. K., & Zawbaa, H. M. (2017). Hybrid Biometrics and Watermarking Authentication. In S. Zoughbi (Ed.), *Securing Government Information and Data in Developing Countries* (pp. 37–61). Hershey, PA: IGI Global. doi:10.4018/978-1-5225-1703-0.ch003

Goher, S. Z., Javed, B., & Bloodsworth, P. (2016). A Survey of Cloud-Based Services Leveraged by Big Data Applications. In R. Kannan, R. Rasool, H. Jin, & S. Balasundaram (Eds.), *Managing and Processing Big Data in Cloud Computing* (pp. 121–131). Hershey, PA: IGI Global. doi:10.4018/978-1-4666-9767-6.ch008

Hallappanavar, V. L., & Birje, M. N. (2017). Trust Management in Cloud Computing. In M. Dawson, M. Eltayeb, & M. Omar (Eds.), *Security Solutions for Hyperconnectivity and the Internet of Things* (pp. 151–183). Hershey, PA: IGI Global. doi:10.4018/978-1-5225-0741-3.ch007

Hamidine, H., & Mahmood, A. (2017). Cloud Computing Data Storage Security Based on Different Encryption Schemes. In J. Chen, Y. Zhang, & R. Gottschalk (Eds.), *Handbook of Research on End-to-End Cloud Computing Architecture Design* (pp. 189–221). Hershey, PA: IGI Global. doi:10.4018/978-1-5225-0759-8.ch009

Hinton, H. (2017). Security and Compliance: IaaS, PaaS, and Hybrid Cloud. In J. Chen, Y. Zhang, & R. Gottschalk (Eds.), *Handbook of Research on End-to-End Cloud Computing Architecture Design* (pp. 159–188). Hershey, PA: IGI Global. doi:10.4018/978-1-5225-0759-8.ch008

Husain, M. S., & Khan, N. (2017). Big Data on E-Government. In S. Zoughbi (Ed.), *Securing Government Information and Data in Developing Countries* (pp. 27–36). Hershey, PA: IGI Global. doi:10.4018/978-1-5225-1703-0.ch002

Husain, M. S., & Khanum, M. A. (2017). Cloud Computing in E-Governance: Indian Perspective. In S. Zoughbi (Ed.), *Securing Government Information and Data in Developing Countries* (pp. 104–114). Hershey, PA: IGI Global. doi:10.4018/978-1-5225-1703-0.ch006

Jadon, K. S., Mudgal, P., & Bhadoria, R. S. (2016). Optimization and Management of Resource in Utility Computing. In G. Deka, G. Siddesh, K. Srinivasa, & L. Patnaik (Eds.), *Emerging Research Surrounding Power Consumption and Performance Issues in Utility Computing* (pp. 22–43). Hershey, PA: IGI Global. doi:10.4018/978-1-4666-8853-7.ch002

Jain, P., & Pang, Y. (2017). Cloud Computing Architectural Patterns. In J. Chen, Y. Zhang, & R. Gottschalk (Eds.), *Handbook of Research on End-to-End Cloud Computing Architecture Design* (pp. 56–72). Hershey, PA: IGI Global. doi:10.4018/978-1-5225-0759-8.ch004

Jaluka, R. (2017). Enterprise IT Transformation Using Cloud Service Broker. In J. Chen, Y. Zhang, & R. Gottschalk (Eds.), *Handbook of Research on End-to-End Cloud Computing Architecture Design* (pp. 348–375). Hershey, PA: IGI Global. doi:10.4018/978-1-5225-0759-8.ch015

Jena, G. C. (2017). Multi-Sensor Data Fusion (MSDF). In N. Ray & A. Turuk (Eds.), *Handbook of Research on Advanced Wireless Sensor Network Applications, Protocols, and Architectures* (pp. 29–61). Hershey, PA: IGI Global. doi:10.4018/978-1-5225-0486-3.ch002

Kasemsap, K. (2017). Robotics: Theory and Applications. In M. Moore (Ed.), *Cybersecurity Breaches and Issues Surrounding Online Threat Protection* (pp. 311–345). Hershey, PA: IGI Global. doi:10.4018/978-1-5225-1941-6.ch013

Khadtare, M. S. (2016). GPU Based Image Quality Assessment using Structural Similarity (SSIM) Index. In G. Deka, G. Siddesh, K. Srinivasa, & L. Patnaik (Eds.), *Emerging Research Surrounding Power Consumption and Performance Issues in Utility Computing* (pp. 276–282). Hershey, PA: IGI Global. doi:10.4018/978-1-4666-8853-7.ch013

Khandelwal, P., & Somani, G. (2017). Virtual Machine Placement in IaaS Cloud. In J. Chen, Y. Zhang, & R. Gottschalk (Eds.), *Handbook of Research on End-to-End Cloud Computing Architecture Design* (pp. 130–158). Hershey, PA: IGI Global. doi:10.4018/978-1-5225-0759-8.ch007

Kiran, M. (2016). Legal Issues Surrounding Connected Government Services: A Closer Look at G-Clouds. In Z. Mahmood (Ed.), *Cloud Computing Technologies for Connected Government* (pp. 322–344). Hershey, PA: IGI Global. doi:10.4018/978-1-4666-8629-8.ch013

Kuada, E. (2017). Security and Trust in Cloud Computing. In M. Dawson, M. Eltayeb, & M. Omar (Eds.), *Security Solutions for Hyperconnectivity and the Internet of Things* (pp. 184–210). Hershey, PA: IGI Global. doi:10.4018/978-1-5225-0741-3.ch008

Kumar, N., & Singh, Y. (2017). Routing Protocols in Wireless Sensor Networks. In N. Ray & A. Turuk (Eds.), *Handbook of Research on Advanced Wireless Sensor Network Applications, Protocols, and Architectures* (pp. 86–128). Hershey, PA: IGI Global. doi:10.4018/978-1-5225-0486-3.ch004

Kumar, V., & Kumar, R. (2017). Prevention of Blackhole Attack using Certificateless Signature (CLS) Scheme in MANET. In M. Dawson, M. Eltayeb, & M. Omar (Eds.), *Security Solutions for Hyperconnectivity and the Internet of Things* (pp. 130–150). Hershey, PA: IGI Global. doi:10.4018/978-1-5225-0741-3.ch006

Lee, J., Eapen, A. M., Akbar, M. S., & Rao, H. R. (2017). An Exploration Regarding Issues in Insider Threat. In M. Moore (Ed.), *Cybersecurity Breaches and Issues Surrounding Online Threat Protection* (pp. 1–23). Hershey, PA: IGI Global. doi:10.4018/978-1-5225-1941-6.ch001

Levy, C. L., & Elias, N. I. (2017). SOHO Users' Perceptions of Reliability and Continuity of Cloud-Based Services. In M. Moore (Ed.), *Cybersecurity Breaches and Issues Surrounding Online Threat Protection* (pp. 248–287). Hershey, PA: IGI Global. doi:10.4018/978-1-5225-1941-6.ch011

Lewis, G. A., Echeverría, S., Simanta, S., Root, J., & Bradshaw, B. (2015). Cloudlet-Based Cyber-Foraging in Resource-Limited Environments. In S. Bagchi (Ed.), *Emerging Research in Cloud Distributed Computing Systems* (pp. 92–121). Hershey, PA: IGI Global. doi:10.4018/978-1-4666-8213-9.ch003

Mahmood, Z. (2016). Cloud Computing Technologies for Open Connected Government. In Z. Mahmood (Ed.), *Cloud Computing Technologies for Connected Government* (pp. 1–14). Hershey, PA: IGI Global. doi:10.4018/978-1-4666-8629-8.ch001

Maiti, P., Addya, S. K., Sahoo, B., & Turuk, A. K. (2017). Energy Efficient Wireless Body Area Network (WBAN). In N. Ray & A. Turuk (Eds.), *Handbook of Research on Advanced Wireless Sensor Network Applications, Protocols, and Architectures* (pp. 413–432). Hershey, PA: IGI Global. doi:10.4018/978-1-5225-0486-3.ch017

Majeed, H., & Erum, F. (2016). Exploiting Semantics to Improve Classification of Text Corpus. In R. Kannan, R. Rasool, H. Jin, & S. Balasundaram (Eds.), *Managing and Processing Big Data in Cloud Computing* (pp. 23–36). Hershey, PA: IGI Global. doi:10.4018/978-1-4666-9767-6.ch002

Manohari, P. K., & Ray, N. K. (2017). A Comprehensive Study of Security in Cloud Computing. In N. Ray & A. Turuk (Eds.), *Handbook of Research on Advanced Wireless Sensor Network Applications, Protocols, and Architectures* (pp. 386–412). Hershey, PA: IGI Global. doi:10.4018/978-1-5225-0486-3.ch016

Manzoor, A. (2016). Cloud Computing Applications in the Public Sector. In Z. Mahmood (Ed.), *Cloud Computing Technologies for Connected Government* (pp. 215–246). Hershey, PA: IGI Global. doi:10.4018/978-1-4666-8629-8.ch009

Marzantowicz, K., & Paciorkowski, Ł. (2017). Community Cloud: Closing the Gap between Public and Private. In J. Chen, Y. Zhang, & R. Gottschalk (Eds.), *Handbook of Research on End-to-End Cloud Computing Architecture Design* (pp. 39–55). Hershey, PA: IGI Global. doi:10.4018/978-1-5225-0759-8.ch003

Meghanathan, N. (2017). Impact of the Structure of the Data Gathering Trees on Node Lifetime and Network Lifetime in Wireless Sensor Networks. In N. Ray & A. Turuk (Eds.), *Handbook of Research on Advanced Wireless Sensor Network Applications, Protocols, and Architectures* (pp. 184–196). Hershey, PA: IGI Global. doi:10.4018/978-1-5225-0486-3.ch007

Memishi, B., Ibrahim, S., Perez, M. S., & Antoniu, G. (2016). On the Dynamic Shifting of the MapReduce Timeout. In R. Kannan, R. Rasool, H. Jin, & S. Balasundaram (Eds.), *Managing and Processing Big Data in Cloud Computing* (pp. 1–22). Hershey, PA: IGI Global. doi:10.4018/978-1-4666-9767-6.ch001

Meralto, C., Moura, J., & Marinheiro, R. (2017). Wireless Mesh Sensor Networks with Mobile Devices: A Comprehensive Review. In N. Ray & A. Turuk (Eds.), *Handbook of Research on Advanced Wireless Sensor Network Applications, Protocols, and Architectures* (pp. 129–155). Hershey, PA: IGI Global. doi:10.4018/978-1-5225-0486-3.ch005

Minto-Coy, I. D., & Henlin, M. G. (2017). The Development of Cybersecurity Policy and Legislative Landscape in Latin America and Caribbean States. In M. Moore (Ed.), *Cybersecurity Breaches and Issues Surrounding Online Threat Protection* (pp. 24–53). Hershey, PA: IGI Global. doi:10.4018/978-1-5225-1941-6.ch002

Mishra, A. K. (2017). Security Threats in Wireless Sensor Networks. In N. Ray & A. Turuk (Eds.), *Handbook of Research on Advanced Wireless Sensor Network Applications, Protocols, and Architectures* (pp. 307–325). Hershey, PA: IGI Global. doi:10.4018/978-1-5225-0486-3.ch012

Mohammed, D., Omar, M., & Nguyen, V. (2017). Enhancing Cyber Security for Financial Industry through Compliance and Regulatory Standards. In M. Dawson, M. Eltayeb, & M. Omar (Eds.), *Security Solutions for Hyperconnectivity and the Internet of Things* (pp. 113–129). Hershey, PA: IGI Global. doi:10.4018/978-1-5225-0741-3.ch005

Mohammed, L. A. (2017). Managing Risk in Cloud Computing. In K. Munir (Ed.), *Security Management in Mobile Cloud Computing* (pp. 73–91). Hershey, PA: IGI Global. doi:10.4018/978-1-5225-0602-7.ch004

Mohanty, J. P., & Mandal, C. (2017). Connected Dominating Set in Wireless Sensor Network. In N. Ray & A. Turuk (Eds.), *Handbook of Research on Advanced Wireless Sensor Network Applications, Protocols, and Architectures* (pp. 62–85). Hershey, PA: IGI Global. doi:10.4018/978-1-5225-0486-3.ch003

Mohanty, R. P., Turuk, A. K., & Sahoo, B. (2016). Designing of High Performance Multicore Processor with Improved Cache Configuration and Interconnect. In G. Deka, G. Siddesh, K. Srinivasa, & L. Patnaik (Eds.), *Emerging Research Surrounding Power Consumption and Performance Issues in Utility Computing* (pp. 204–219). Hershey, PA: IGI Global. doi:10.4018/978-1-4666-8853-7.ch009

Mohanty, S., Patra, P. K., & Mohapatra, S. (2016). Dynamic Task Assignment with Load Balancing in Cloud Platform. In G. Deka, G. Siddesh, K. Srinivasa, & L. Patnaik (Eds.), *Emerging Research Surrounding Power Consumption and Performance Issues in Utility Computing* (pp. 363–385). Hershey, PA: IGI Global. doi:10.4018/978-1-4666-8853-7.ch018

Mohanty, S., & Patra, S. K. (2017). Performance Evaluation of Quality of Service in IEEE 802.15.4-Based Wireless Sensor Networks. In N. Ray & A. Turuk (Eds.), *Handbook of Research on Advanced Wireless Sensor Network Applications, Protocols, and Architectures* (pp. 213–248). Hershey, PA: IGI Global. doi:10.4018/978-1-5225-0486-3.ch009

Mosthaf, J., & Wagner, H. (2016). The Architects Role in Business-IT Alignment. *International Journal of IT/Business Alignment and Governance*, *7*(1), 36–49. doi:10.4018/IJITBAG.2016010103

Mrozek, D. (2015). Cloud-Based Computing Architectures for Solving Hot Issues in Structural Bioinformatics. In S. Bagchi (Ed.), *Emerging Research in Cloud Distributed Computing Systems* (pp. 294–314). Hershey, PA: IGI Global. doi:10.4018/978-1-4666-8213-9.ch009

Mukherjee, S., Geethapriya, R., & Surianarayanan, S. (2016). A Cloud-Based Framework for Connected Governance. In Z. Mahmood (Ed.), *Cloud Computing Technologies for Connected Government* (pp. 94–123). Hershey, PA: IGI Global. doi:10.4018/978-1-4666-8629-8.ch005

Munir, K. (2017). Security Model for Mobile Cloud Database as a Service (DBaaS). In K. Munir (Ed.), *Security Management in Mobile Cloud Computing* (pp. 169–180). Hershey, PA: IGI Global. doi:10.4018/978-1-5225-0602-7.ch008

Mwirigi, G. B., Zo, H., Rho, J. J., & Park, M. J. (2017). An Empirical Investigation of M-Government Acceptance in Developing Countries: A Case of Kenya. In S. Zoughbi (Ed.), *Securing Government Information and Data in Developing Countries* (pp. 62–89). Hershey, PA: IGI Global. doi:10.4018/978-1-5225-1703-0.ch004

Narayanapppa, M. T., Channabasamma, A., & Hegadi, R. S. (2016). Need of Hadoop and Map Reduce for Processing and Managing Big Data. In R. Kannan, R. Rasool, H. Jin, & S. Balasundaram (Eds.), *Managing and Processing Big Data in Cloud Computing* (pp. 132–144). Hershey, PA: IGI Global. doi:10.4018/978-1-4666-9767-6.ch009

Narayanapppa, M. T., Kumar, T. P., & Hegadi, R. S. (2016). Essentiality of Machine Learning Algorithms for Big Data Computation. In R. Kannan, R. Rasool, H. Jin, & S. Balasundaram (Eds.), *Managing and Processing Big Data in Cloud Computing* (pp. 156–167). Hershey, PA: IGI Global. doi:10.4018/978-1-4666-9767-6.ch011

Nawaz, S., Malik, A. W., & ur Rasool, R. (2016). Ceaseless Virtual Appliance Streaming: Creation and Transmission of Virtual Packs over Network. In R. Kannan, R. Rasool, H. Jin, & S. Balasundaram (Eds.), *Managing and Processing Big Data in Cloud Computing* (pp. 70-84). Hershey, PA: IGI Global. doi:10.4018/978-1-4666-9767-6.ch005

Nayak, P. (2017). Internet of Things Services, Applications, Issues, and Challenges. In N. Ray & A. Turuk (Eds.), *Handbook of Research on Advanced Wireless Sensor Network Applications, Protocols, and Architectures* (pp. 353–368). Hershey, PA: IGI Global. doi:10.4018/978-1-5225-0486-3.ch014

Nobles, C. (2017). Cyber Threats in Civil Aviation. In M. Dawson, M. Eltayeb, & M. Omar (Eds.), *Security Solutions for Hyperconnectivity and the Internet of Things* (pp. 272–301). Hershey, PA: IGI Global. doi:10.4018/978-1-5225-0741-3.ch011

Omar, M., Ahmad, K., & Rizvi, M. (2016). Content Based Image Retrieval System. In G. Deka, G. Siddesh, K. Srinivasa, & L. Patnaik (Eds.), *Emerging Research Surrounding Power Consumption and Performance Issues in Utility Computing* (pp. 345–362). Hershey, PA: IGI Global. doi:10.4018/978-1-4666-8853-7.ch017

Panda, S. (2017). Security Issues and Challenges in Internet of Things. In N. Ray & A. Turuk (Eds.), *Handbook of Research on Advanced Wireless Sensor Network Applications, Protocols, and Architectures* (pp. 369–385). Hershey, PA: IGI Global. doi:10.4018/978-1-5225-0486-3.ch015

Pang, C. (2016). An Agile Architecture for a Legacy Enterprise IT System. *International Journal of Organizational and Collective Intelligence*, *6*(4), 65–97. doi:10.4018/IJOCI.2016100104

Piraghaj, S. F., Dastjerdi, A. V., Calheiros, R. N., & Buyya, R. (2017). A Survey and Taxonomy of Energy Efficient Resource Management Techniques in Platform as a Service Cloud. In J. Chen, Y. Zhang, & R. Gottschalk (Eds.), *Handbook of Research on End-to-End Cloud Computing Architecture Design* (pp. 410–454). Hershey, PA: IGI Global. doi:10.4018/978-1-5225-0759-8.ch017

Pop, D., Echeverria, A., Petcu, D., & Conesa, G. (2016). Enabling Open and Collaborative Public Service Advertising through Cloud Technologies. In Z. Mahmood (Ed.), *Cloud Computing Technologies for Connected Government* (pp. 269–290). Hershey, PA: IGI Global. doi:10.4018/978-1-4666-8629-8.ch011

Posea, I., Ion, M., Pop, F., Popescu, D., & Popescu, N. (2016). E-Vote: A Cloud-Based Electronic Voting System for Large-Scale Election. In Z. Mahmood (Ed.), *Cloud Computing Technologies for Connected Government* (pp. 188–213). Hershey, PA: IGI Global. doi:10.4018/978-1-4666-8629-8.ch008

Prusty, A. R., Sethi, S., & Nayak, A. K. (2017). Energy Aware Optimized Routing Protocols for Wireless Ad Hoc Sensor Network. In N. Ray & A. Turuk (Eds.), *Handbook of Research on Advanced Wireless Sensor Network Applications, Protocols, and Architectures* (pp. 156–183). Hershey, PA: IGI Global. doi:10.4018/978-1-5225-0486-3.ch006

Qamar, M., Malik, M., Batool, S., Mehmood, S., Malik, A. W., & Rahman, A. (2016). Centralized to Decentralized Social Networks: Factors that Matter. In R. Kannan, R. Rasool, H. Jin, & S. Balasundaram (Eds.), *Managing and Processing Big Data in Cloud Computing* (pp. 37–54). Hershey, PA: IGI Global. doi:10.4018/978-1-4666-9767-6.ch003

Raj, P. (2016). Significance of Clouds for Connected Governments: The Government Clouds in India. In Z. Mahmood (Ed.), *Cloud Computing Technologies for Connected Government* (pp. 15–38). Hershey, PA: IGI Global. doi:10.4018/978-1-4666-8629-8.ch002

Richardson, L., & Mukherjea, S. (2017). Enterprise Mobility Reference Architecture: Mobility Services Overview. In J. Chen, Y. Zhang, & R. Gottschalk (Eds.), *Handbook of Research on End-to-End Cloud Computing Architecture Design* (pp. 1–14). Hershey, PA: IGI Global. doi:10.4018/978-1-5225-0759-8.ch001

Rouhani, B. D., Mahrin, M. N., Shirazi, H., Nikpay, F., & Rouhani, B. D. (2015). An Effectiveness Model for Enterprise Architecture Methodologies. *International Journal of Enterprise Information Systems*, *11*(2), 50–64. doi:10.4018/IJEIS.2015040103

Rout, S., Turuk, A. K., & Sahoo, B. (2017). Techniques to Enhance the Lifetime of MANET. In N. Ray & A. Turuk (Eds.), *Handbook of Research on Advanced Wireless Sensor Network Applications, Protocols, and Architectures* (pp. 278–306). Hershey, PA: IGI Global. doi:10.4018/978-1-5225-0486-3.ch011

S., S., & R., P. (2017). Cybercrime Investigation. In M. Moore (Ed.), *Cybersecurity Breaches and Issues Surrounding Online Threat Protection* (pp. 96-120). Hershey, PA: IGI Global. doi:10.4018/978-1-5225-1941-6.ch005

S., T., & Pahwa, B. (2017). Empowering IT with Green Computing. In N. Ray, & A. Turuk (Eds.), *Handbook of Research on Advanced Wireless Sensor Network Applications, Protocols, and Architectures* (pp. 433-450). Hershey, PA: IGI Global. doi:10.4018/978-1-5225-0486-3.ch018

Schmeida, M., & McNeal, R. S. (2017). Internet Pharmacy Cybercrime: State Policy Mitigating Risks 2000-2015. In M. Moore (Ed.), *Cybersecurity Breaches and Issues Surrounding Online Threat Protection* (pp. 54–73). Hershey, PA: IGI Global. doi:10.4018/978-1-5225-1941-6.ch003

Sen, J. (2014). Security and Privacy Issues in Cloud Computing. In A. Ruiz-Martinez, R. Marin-Lopez, & F. Pereniguez-Garcia (Eds.), *Architectures and Protocols for Secure Information Technology Infrastructures* (pp. 1–45). Hershey, PA: IGI Global. doi:10.4018/978-1-4666-4514-1.ch001

Sethi, S., & Sahoo, R. K. (2017). Design of WSN in Real Time Application of Health Monitoring System. In N. Ray & A. Turuk (Eds.), *Handbook of Research on Advanced Wireless Sensor Network Applications, Protocols, and Architectures* (pp. 197–212). Hershey, PA: IGI Global. doi:10.4018/978-1-5225-0486-3.ch008

Shalan, M. A. (2017). Considering Middle Circles in Mobile Cloud Computing: Ethics and Risk Governance. In K. Munir (Ed.), *Security Management in Mobile Cloud Computing* (pp. 43–72). Hershey, PA: IGI Global. doi:10.4018/978-1-5225-0602-7.ch003

Shalan, M. A. (2017). Risk and Governance Considerations in Cloud Era. In J. Chen, Y. Zhang, & R. Gottschalk (Eds.), *Handbook of Research on End-to-End Cloud Computing Architecture Design* (pp. 376–409). Hershey, PA: IGI Global. doi:10.4018/978-1-5225-0759-8.ch016

Shamsolmoali, P., Zareapoor, M., & Alam, M. (2017). Multi-Aspect DDOS Detection System for Securing Cloud Network. In J. Chen, Y. Zhang, & R. Gottschalk (Eds.), *Handbook of Research on End-to-End Cloud Computing Architecture Design* (pp. 222–252). Hershey, PA: IGI Global. doi:10.4018/978-1-5225-0759-8.ch010

Shawish, A., & Salama, M. (2015). Cloud-Based Healthcare Systems: Emerging Technologies and Open Research Issues. In S. Bagchi (Ed.), *Emerging Research in Cloud Distributed Computing Systems* (pp. 315–338). Hershey, PA: IGI Global. doi:10.4018/978-1-4666-8213-9.ch010

Shen, L., Chen, I., & Su, A. (2017). Cybersecurity and Data Breaches at Schools. In M. Moore (Ed.), *Cybersecurity Breaches and Issues Surrounding Online Threat Protection* (pp. 144–174). Hershey, PA: IGI Global. doi:10.4018/978-1-5225-1941-6.ch007

Silva, N., Ferreira, F., Sousa, P., & Mira da Silva, M. (2016). Automating the Migration of Enterprise Architecture Models. *International Journal of Information System Modeling and Design*, *7*(2), 72–90. doi:10.4018/IJISMD.2016040104

Singh, B., & K.S., J. (2017). Security Management in Mobile Cloud Computing: Security and Privacy Issues and Solutions in Mobile Cloud Computing. In K. Munir (Ed.), *Security Management in Mobile Cloud Computing* (pp. 148-168). Hershey, PA: IGI Global. doi:10.4018/978-1-5225-0602-7.ch007

Singh, S., & Gond, S. (2016). Green Computing and Its Impact. In G. Deka, G. Siddesh, K. Srinivasa, & L. Patnaik (Eds.), *Emerging Research Surrounding Power Consumption and Performance Issues in Utility Computing* (pp. 69–83). Hershey, PA: IGI Global. doi:10.4018/978-1-4666-8853-7.ch004

Sivagurunathan, S., & Swasthimathi, L. S. (2016). Cloud Computing Applications in Education through E-Governance: An Indian Perspective. In Z. Mahmood (Ed.), *Cloud Computing Technologies for Connected Government* (pp. 247–268). Hershey, PA: IGI Global. doi:10.4018/978-1-4666-8629-8.ch010

Srinivasa, K. G., Hegde, G., Sideesh, G. M., & Hiriyannaiah, S. (2016). A Viability Analysis of an Economical Private Cloud Storage Solution Powered by Raspberry Pi in the NSA Era: A Survey and Analysis of Cost and Security. In G. Deka, G. Siddesh, K. Srinivasa, & L. Patnaik (Eds.), *Emerging Research Surrounding Power Consumption and Performance Issues in Utility Computing* (pp. 220–232). Hershey, PA: IGI Global. doi:10.4018/978-1-4666-8853-7.ch010

Srinivasa, K. G., Siddesh, G. M., Hiriyannaiah, S., Mishra, K., Prajeeth, C. S., & Talha, A. M. (2016). GPU Implementation of Friend Recommendation System using CUDA for Social Networking Services. In G. Deka, G. Siddesh, K. Srinivasa, & L. Patnaik (Eds.), *Emerging Research Surrounding Power Consumption and Performance Issues in Utility Computing* (pp. 304–319). Hershey, PA: IGI Global. doi:10.4018/978-1-4666-8853-7.ch015

Susanto, H., & Almunawar, M. N. (2016). Security and Privacy Issues in Cloud-Based E-Government. In Z. Mahmood (Ed.), *Cloud Computing Technologies for Connected Government* (pp. 292–321). Hershey, PA: IGI Global. doi:10.4018/978-1-4666-8629-8.ch012

Suthakar, K. I., & Devi, M. K. (2016). Resource Scheduling for Big Data on Cloud: Scheduling Resources. In R. Kannan, R. Rasool, H. Jin, & S. Balasundaram (Eds.), *Managing and Processing Big Data in Cloud Computing* (pp. 185–205). Hershey, PA: IGI Global. doi:10.4018/978-1-4666-9767-6.ch013

Swarnkar, M., & Bhadoria, R. S. (2016). Security Aspects in Utility Computing. In G. Deka, G. Siddesh, K. Srinivasa, & L. Patnaik (Eds.), *Emerging Research Surrounding Power Consumption and Performance Issues in Utility Computing* (pp. 262–275). Hershey, PA: IGI Global. doi:10.4018/978-1-4666-8853-7.ch012

Tank, D. M. (2017). Security and Privacy Issues, Solutions, and Tools for MCC. In K. Munir (Ed.), *Security Management in Mobile Cloud Computing* (pp. 121–147). Hershey, PA: IGI Global. doi:10.4018/978-1-5225-0602-7.ch006

Thio, C., & Cook, J. (2017). Workload Migration to Cloud. In J. Chen, Y. Zhang, & R. Gottschalk (Eds.), *Handbook of Research on End-to-End Cloud Computing Architecture Design* (pp. 279–298). Hershey, PA: IGI Global. doi:10.4018/978-1-5225-0759-8.ch012

Thota, C., Manogaran, G., Lopez, D., & Vijayakumar, V. (2017). Big Data Security Framework for Distributed Cloud Data Centers. In M. Moore (Ed.), *Cybersecurity Breaches and Issues Surrounding Online Threat Protection* (pp. 288–310). Hershey, PA: IGI Global. doi:10.4018/978-1-5225-1941-6.ch012

Trad, A., & Kalpić, D. (2015). The Business Transformation Framework for Managers in Business Innovation Transformation Projects: Business Architecture Managerial Recommendation. *International Journal of Human Capital and Information Technology Professionals*, *6*(4), 22–45. doi:10.4018/IJHCITP.2015100102

Umair, S., Muneer, U., Zahoor, M. N., & Malik, A. W. (2016). Mobile Cloud Computing Future Trends and Opportunities. In R. Kannan, R. Rasool, H. Jin, & S. Balasundaram (Eds.), *Managing and Processing Big Data in Cloud Computing* (pp. 105–120). Hershey, PA: IGI Global. doi:10.4018/978-1-4666-9767-6.ch007

Venkata, M. G., & Poole, S. (2015). Parallel Programming Models and Systems for High Performance Computing. In S. Bagchi (Ed.), *Emerging Research in Cloud Distributed Computing Systems* (pp. 254–292). Hershey, PA: IGI Global. doi:10.4018/978-1-4666-8213-9.ch008

Venkateswaran, S. (2017). Industrial Patterns on Cloud. In J. Chen, Y. Zhang, & R. Gottschalk (Eds.), *Handbook of Research on End-to-End Cloud Computing Architecture Design* (pp. 73–103). Hershey, PA: IGI Global. doi:10.4018/978-1-5225-0759-8.ch005

Wolfe, M. (2017). Establishing Governance for Hybrid Cloud and the Internet of Things. In J. Chen, Y. Zhang, & R. Gottschalk (Eds.), *Handbook of Research on End-to-End Cloud Computing Architecture Design* (pp. 300–325). Hershey, PA: IGI Global. doi:10.4018/978-1-5225-0759-8.ch013

Yahaya, M. O. (2017). On the Role of Game Theory in Modelling Incentives and Interactions in Mobile Distributed Systems. In K. Munir (Ed.), *Security Management in Mobile Cloud Computing* (pp. 92–120). Hershey, PA: IGI Global. doi:10.4018/978-1-5225-0602-7.ch005

Zaibi, G., Peyrard, F., Kachouri, A., Fournier-Prunaret, D., & Samet, M. (2014). A New Encryption Algorithm based on Chaotic Map for Wireless Sensor Network. In A. Ruiz-Martinez, R. Marin-Lopez, & F. Pereniguez-Garcia (Eds.), *Architectures and Protocols for Secure Information Technology Infrastructures* (pp. 103–123). Hershey, PA: IGI Global. doi:10.4018/978-1-4666-4514-1.ch004

Zhang, W., Qi, Q., & Deng, J. (2017). Building Intelligent Transportation Cloud Data Center Based on SOA. *International Journal of Ambient Computing and Intelligence*, *8*(2), 1–11. doi:10.4018/IJACI.2017040101

Zhao, Q., Ma, M., Zhang, Y., & He, B. (2015). Access Control in Cloud Computing. In S. Bagchi (Ed.), *Emerging Research in Cloud Distributed Computing Systems* (pp. 340–362). Hershey, PA: IGI Global. doi:10.4018/978-1-4666-8213-9.ch011

Zolotow, C., Graf, F., Pfitzmann, B., Huber, R., Schlatter, M., Schrøder-Hansen, C., & Hunt, A. (2017). Transition and Transformation into a Cloud Environment. In J. Chen, Y. Zhang, & R. Gottschalk (Eds.), *Handbook of Research on End-to-End Cloud Computing Architecture Design* (pp. 254–278). Hershey, PA: IGI Global. doi:10.4018/978-1-5225-0759-8.ch011

Zoughbi, S. (2017). Major Issues Affecting Government Data and Information in Developing Countries. In S. Zoughbi (Ed.), *Securing Government Information and Data in Developing Countries* (pp. 115–126). Hershey, PA: IGI Global. doi:10.4018/978-1-5225-1703-0.ch007

Zoughbi, S. (2017). Major Technology Trends Affecting Government Data in Developing Countries. In S. Zoughbi (Ed.), *Securing Government Information and Data in Developing Countries* (pp. 127–135). Hershey, PA: IGI Global. doi:10.4018/978-1-5225-1703-0.ch008

About the Author

Amit Tiwary has over three decades' experience in developing pragmatic, implementable enterprise architecture solutions for customers such as Simplot, Telstra, Origin, CBA, Australia taxation office and multiple other organisations. Amit recently implemented an enterprise and business architecture framework for a large organisation that has proved to be an extremely valuable communication device, and has been further developed with subsequent Enterprise Architecture initiatives. He is currently working with a government organisation to establish an enterprise architecture framework with business oriented architectural principles and governance processes. Amit has also delivered multiple workshops and lunch time sessions on various management and information technology topics. In the past he has also been a sessional lecture for postgraduate courses at RMIT, specialising in enterprise architecture.

Index

www.ingramcontent.com/pod-product-compliance
Ingram Content Group UK Ltd.
Pitfield, Milton Keynes, MK11 3LW, UK
UKHW050945290926
15470UKWH00005B/1638

9 781522 524076